The Healing Stories of Jesus

Signs of the New Creation

Louis Grams

the WORD among us® press

Published by The Word Among Us Press
7115 Guilford Drive
Frederick, Maryland 21704
www.wau.org

ISBN: 978-1-59325-290-8

Nihil Obstat:
Msgr. Michael Morgan, J.D., J.C.L., Censor Librorum
April 1, 2016

Imprimatur:
Most Reverend Felipe J. Estévez, Bishop of St. Augustine
April 1, 2016

Scripture texts used in this work are taken from the New Revised Standard
Version Bible: Catholic Edition, copyright © 1965 and 1966 by the Division of
Christian Education of the National Council of the Churches of Christ in the USA.
All rights reserved. Used with permission.

Excerpts from the English translation of the *Catechism of the Catholic Church*
for use in the United States of America, copyright © 1994, United States Catholic
Conference, Inc.—Libreria Editrice Vaticana. Used with permission.

Cover design by Andrea Alvarez
Cover Art: Jesus healing Peter's mother-in-law (wall painting), Goul, Philippos
(fl.1494) / Church of St. Mamas, Louvaras, Cyprus / Sonia Halliday Photographs /
Bridgeman Images

The contemporary healing stories in this Bible study are all factual. However,
the names and locations have been changed to respect the privacy of each person.

Made and printed in the United States of America

Library of Congress Control Number: 2016936898

Contents

Welcome to
The Word Among Us
Keys to the Bible

Have you ever lost your keys? Everyone seems to have at least one "lost keys" story to tell. Maybe you had to break a window of your house or wait for the auto club to let you into your car. Whatever you had to do probably cost you—in time, energy, money, or all three. Keys are definitely important items to have on hand!

The guides in The Word Among Us Keys to the Bible series are meant to provide you with a handy set of keys that can "unlock" the treasures of the Scriptures for you. Scripture is God's living word. Within its pages we meet the Lord. So as we study and meditate on Scripture and unlock its many treasures, we discover the riches it contains—and in the process, we grow in intimacy with God.

Since 1982 *The Word Among Us* magazine has helped Catholics develop a deeper relationship with the Lord through daily meditations that bring the Scriptures to life. More than ever, Catholics today desire to read and pray with the Scriptures, and many have begun to form small faith-sharing groups to explore the Bible together.

We designed the Keys to the Bible series after conducting a survey among our magazine readers to learn what they would want in a Catholic Bible study. We found that they were looking for easy-to-understand, faith-filled materials that approach Scripture from a clearly Catholic perspective. Moreover, they wanted a Bible study that shows them how they can apply what they learn from Scripture to their everyday lives. They also asked for sessions that they could complete in an hour or two.

Our goal was to design a simple, easy-to-use Bible study guide that is also challenging and thought provoking. We hope that this guide fulfills those admittedly ambitious goals. We are confident, however,

that taking the time to go through this guide—whether by yourself, with a friend, or in a small group—will be a worthwhile endeavor that will bear fruit in your life.

How to Use the Guides in This Series

The study guides in the Keys to the Bible series are divided into six sessions that each deal with a particular aspect of the topic. Before starting the first session, take the time to read the introduction, which sets the stage for the session that follows.

Whether you use this guide for personal reflection and study, as part of a faith-sharing group, or as an aid in your prayer time, be sure to begin each session with prayer. Ask God to open his word to you and to speak to you personally. Read each Scripture passage slowly and carefully. Then, take as much time as you need to meditate on the passage and pursue any thoughts it brings to mind. When you are ready, move on to the accompanying commentary, which offers various insights into the text.

Two sets of questions are included in each session to help you "mine" the Scripture passage and discover its relevance to your life. Those under the heading "Understand!" focus on the text itself and help you grasp what it means. Occasionally a question allows for a variety of answers and is meant to help you explore the passage from several angles. "Grow!" questions are intended to elicit a personal response by helping you examine your life in light of the values and truths that you uncover through your study of the Scripture passage and its setting. Under the headings "Reflect!" and "Act!" we offer suggestions to help you respond concretely to the challenges posed by the passage.

Finally, stories of contemporary healings appear throughout each session. Coupled with relevant selections from the *Catechism of the Catholic Church* and information about the history, geography, and culture of first-century Palestine, these selections (called "In the Spotlight") add new layers of understanding and insight to your study.

As is true with any learning resource, you will benefit the most from this study by writing your answers to the questions in the spaces provided. The simple act of writing can help you formulate your thoughts more clearly—and will also give you a record of your reflections and spiritual growth that you can return to in the future to see how much God has accomplished in your life. End your reading or study with a prayer thanking God for what you have learned—and ask the Holy Spirit to guide you in living out the call you have been given as a Christian in the world today.

Although the Scripture passages to be studied and the related verses for your reflection are printed in full in each guide (from the New Revised Standard Version: Catholic Edition), you will find it helpful to have a Bible on hand for looking up other passages and cross-references or for comparing different translations.

The format of the guides in The Word Among Us Keys to the Bible series is especially well suited for use in small groups. Some recommendations and practical tips for using this guide in a Bible discussion group are offered on pages 98–101.

We hope that this guide will help you to understand the role healing plays in heralding the coming of the kingdom of God and to be open to Jesus' healing presence in your life and in the lives of those around you.

The Word Among Us Press

Introduction
A New Creation Is Coming

There is a certain sense of irony for me in writing this volume of the Keys to the Bible series. On the one hand, I have personally experienced the healing power of Jesus in my own life and have witnessed it in the lives of many other people as well. This healing power has manifested itself in concrete, doctor-certified, physical healing, in marvelous personal transformations, in the repair of damaged relationships, and in many other forms of healing.

I've personally been brought back from death's door as I contended with heart failure, complete renal failure, respiratory failure, and a host of other complications related to a rare autoimmune disorder. In a series of amazing events, the Lord healed me completely of this "incurable" disorder, and I have remained free of any traces of that disease since mid-1997.

On the other hand, I have also lived for long periods of time with chronic disease and pain. I have been frequently prayed for and prayed with, without any apparent sign of physical change or improvement. As I write this, I am several years into experiencing a form of autonomic nervous system failure that has slowly placed increasing physical limits on my daily life and activity. Literally hundreds of people have been faithfully praying for my healing for more than eight years. I experience great grace every day, but while the disease process has slowed, the reality is that it continues to progress.

A longtime friend of mine once said to me, "You know, God has done some astonishing works of healing in you, but for most of the time I've known you, you've been sick. What do you make of that?"

Indeed, what do we make of sickness and pain in our lives? We turn to God and ask him, "Why?" or we grit our teeth and call out to the Lord, asking that we might "know Christ and the power of

his resurrection and the sharing of his sufferings" (Philippians 3:10). And when we ourselves or someone close to us is in the depths of sickness, we ask God for mercy, or that his will would be done, or, perhaps, that he might bring healing in this case.

A New Heaven and a New Earth

If we turn to Scripture, it is impossible to read through the Gospels or Acts of the Apostles without again and again seeing stories of Jesus and his disciples healing the sick. The announcement of the arrival of the kingdom of God is tied to the manifestations of healing and deliverance (see Luke 4:16-21). They are signs of greater things yet to come. There is a new creation—a new heaven and a new earth—that is on its way, and we can taste it even now.

More astonishing, Jesus declares,

> "Very truly, I tell you, the one who believes in me will also do the works that I do and, in fact, will do greater works than these, because I am going to the Father. I will do whatever you ask in my name, so that the Father may be glorified in the Son. If in my name you ask me for anything, I will do it." (John 14:12-14)

And so we read stories of the lives of the saints and find numerous accounts of healing at their hands and beg for their intercession. We can visit one of the great shrines, such as Lourdes, known for the countless cures that have taken place there. We can attend a healing rally or service and see people healed.

But more often than not, when we are ill, we remain in our sickbed, hoping that the pills from the doctor will work or that the surgery will go well, and we nod appreciation when someone tells us that they will pray for us. Signs of the new creation seem very far from us.

If we pray for someone and ask God to heal them, we often give our prayer this precautionary addition: "But do whatever your will is, Lord." We do this both out of humility before God and as a bit of "cover" in case we don't get the answer we are hoping for.

Not everyone who goes to Lourdes or some other pilgrimage destination is healed. Not everyone who goes to a healing Mass or prayer meeting is healed. Not every person who gets prayed with by internationally known healers is healed. Not everyone we pray for is healed, but more often than we might realize, healing as a result of prayer does happen.

We live in an era of advanced medical technology, skill, and technique, but even the best that medicine offers does not always bring healing. Medicine remains something of an art. It is a well-documented, scientifically enriched art, but its outcomes are still not fully predictable.

As followers of Jesus the healer, our efforts to do as he did—to pray with others for healing—are often hesitant and uncertain. Healing is even more of an art than medicine, and when we attempt it, we may feel we as if we are in over our heads.

Our society is at best skeptical of overly simple "spiritual" solutions to problems of health and mortality. In many circles, simply mentioning the possibility of God healing someone raises eyebrows and may generate knowing snickers. Even if we believe that God still does perform miracles, we have our own sense of caution that holds us back from getting our hopes up too high when prayer is proposed as an avenue to healing.

Scripture has much to say to us about suffering, healing, and confronting death. However, in our often cynical age, the stories of healing offered to us in Scripture are often minimized, explained away, or treated as "that was then, this is now" matters that have no particular significance for us today. The ways in which Scripture addresses suffering and death are often viewed as "useful insights" or "words of consolation." Well and good, but those who suffer mightily often find that they need more than consolation!

Jesus in Action

The following study is a meditative exploration of some of the healing stories of Jesus. It is certainly not exhaustive. The New Testament overflows with healing stories and a new way of seeing the place of suffering in our lives. You will not find any formulas for healing here, but you will see Jesus and his disciples in action, bringing healing to others and dealing with pain and struggle in their own lives.

Perhaps as a result, you will find an avenue to greater faith and expectation in the power of God to heal here and now. Perhaps you will find in yourself the heart to accept the power of the Holy Spirit that was planted in you at your baptism and deepened in confirmation. Perhaps you will find the humility and grace to accept God's free and unconditional gifts and step out to use them in love for those around you.

Perhaps too, if you are in need of healing, you will find encouragement to seek out others who will pray with you in faith.

For me, this is a highly personal experience, because of my own repeated experience of physical healing in my own life, because I have seen thousands of instances of physical healing in others, but most of all because the Gospels and the Acts of the Apostles overflow with stories of healing. Healing is a part of the continuing establishment of the reign of God. It is a profound part of the history of the Church. It is a sign of things yet to come.

There is a new creation coming, and it is unfolding in our lives even now.

The Kingdom of God Is Arriving

Luke 4:38-41

³⁸ After leaving the synagogue he entered Simon's house. Now Simon's mother-in-law was suffering from a high fever, and they asked him about her. ³⁹ Then he stood over her and rebuked the fever, and it left her. Immediately she got up and began to serve them.

⁴⁰ As the sun was setting, all those who had any who were sick with various kinds of diseases brought them to him; and he laid his hands on each of them and cured them. ⁴¹ Demons also came out of many, shouting, "You are the Son of God!" But he rebuked them and would not allow them to speak, because they knew that he was the Messiah.

This simple little story of first, the healing of Simon Peter's mother-in-law and then, a flood of other cures falls early in the picture that Luke draws of Jesus' public ministry. Jesus comes out of his time of testing in the wilderness and makes a bold declaration of his ministry as he reads from the scroll of Isaiah in the synagogue. At once there is both awe and outrage. His neighbors want him dead (Luke 4:16-29)!

Jesus manages to pass through the angry crowd and travel to Capernaum, where he begins to teach in the synagogue. People are astounded by the authority with which he speaks. A confrontation with a demoniac in which the demon proclaims Jesus to be "the Holy One of God" (Luke 4:34) causes even more wonder among the people, and word quickly starts to spread that something new is happening.

Let's walk with Jesus over to Simon's house. Jesus has just finished teaching in the synagogue. A crowd buzzing with animated

conversation follows him right to the door, but Jesus goes inside, where he finds Simon's mother-in-law sick with a fever. She is in bed, burning up in a dark corner of the room. She is too sick to move or attempt to get up to serve her unexpected guest.

The family worriedly tells Jesus about her condition. His response is immediate and simple. He goes to her side and rebukes the fever. For a moment, the family members who are present are confused by this blunt act. Is he mocking the poor woman?

But there is no mockery in what he has done. The fever instantly leaves Simon's mother-in-law. No sooner is she freed than she is out of bed and hard at work, preparing food for her family and guest, tidying things up, quietly fussing over everyone the way only a very good hostess can. Her house is full; she must serve.

Everyone is stunned by what they have just seen. The woman was so sick that she could not lift a finger to welcome her guests, and now she is serving them as though nothing had ever been wrong with her. She takes it all in stride. There is no time for wonder. She has work to do!

The wonders, however, are just beginning. As the afternoon fades into evening, word of what has happened circulates beyond the house. To some, the story seems preposterous or, at best, unlikely. But for many, the sense is "This is what we have been waiting for!" They have been taught over the centuries to expect one to come who would bring life and healing. The crowds gather up everyone they can think of who has any kind of sickness or disability.

Jesus steps out of the house and into the crowd and begins to lay hands on each of the sick, and one by one, they are all cured on the spot. With each healing, the excitement and expectation in the crowd grow. Those being healed are family members and

friends. Many have been sick for years, and in a moment, they are made whole.

Finally, night settles on the village. The people go to their homes. Jesus has had a very full day of ministry. He has brought the "good news to the poor." He has proclaimed "release to the captives," given "sight to the blind," and "let the oppressed go free" (Luke 4:18).

The year of favor that Isaiah had promised so long ago, and that all of Israel hoped to see, has arrived. Suddenly, God is at work in the world, making all things new, creating a new earth and a new heaven. The shift in the course of history has begun.

The old covenant expectations between God and his people are being fulfilled and completed, and even as that covenant is sealed, a new covenant with new expectations is being introduced that will culminate in resurrected life, first in Jesus and then in all who believe in him. In the new creation, sickness and pain will be overcome, death itself will be vanquished, and even now we can see it happening.

In the Gospel of Luke, this day of teaching and healing is the launching point for many more days filled with teaching, healing, and even the raising of the dead. Jesus demonstrates the power and love of God and shows us glimpses of the future he has in store for all who follow him. He lets us see the beginning moments of a new creation that is still unfolding and will be completed on the day when he is "all in all" (1 Corinthians 15:28).

This new creation is still very much in process. God is at work in our lives. We may not always be alert to his presence and action, but he continues to come to us with mercy, forgiveness, healing, and new life, and he wants our lives to be filled with hopeful expectation.

I still remember a presentation given in our parish when I was only a young boy. A priest who was traveling from parish to parish showed a film and told stories about Padre Pio, who was very much alive at the time. Not only did he talk about the mystery of Padre Pio's stigmata but also about the signs and wonders that were happening around him, including physical healing.

I also remember a trip to the shrine of St. Anne de Beaupré in Quebec, Canada. Leaning against the walls of the vestibule of the church were crutches, stretchers, and braces of all kinds, all of which had been left there by people who had come to the shrine and had been physically healed. Of course, I knew the stories of Lourdes and St. Bernadette. We watched the film of her life at school. We also watched the film about the apparitions at Fatima.

For me, the notion that God is still working wonders of healing and transformation in our own time did not seem surprising. Why would he not be doing that?

I later went through a time during which I was far more skeptical, but as my teenage years drew to a close, I found myself drawn to make a commitment of my life to Jesus. I had been poring over the Scriptures, and gradually they were coming alive to me. A wise teacher taught me how to meditate on scenes from the life of Jesus and to enter into those scenes, not just as an observer, but as a participant.

The more I knew Jesus as a person, the more it seemed that he was not just a wonderful figure in the past, nor simply a mysterious, silent presence in the tabernacle; he was active and present in the people and experiences of daily life. I became more and more aware of the tangible ways in which his love continues to be manifested in the world and more expectant of what that love could accomplish. When I first encountered people who believe wholeheartedly that

Jesus continues to heal people, not only at the great shrines but among ordinary people simply because they ask him to, I was not surprised. It made sense. I even expected it. After all, Jesus himself had said that those who believe in him would be able to do such things (see Mark 16:17-18; John 14:12-14).

The disciples expected such healings and performed them. I began to expect to see healing happen simply because people were moved in faith to ask for it. It was not a commonplace thing, and I could not tell why it would happen in some cases and not in others. But I did see it happen, and it just seemed right—exactly what Jesus had promised.

Understand

1. Jesus "rebuked" the fever that was plaguing Peter's mother-in-law, just as he rebuked the demons. What does that imply about her illness?

   We felt hopeless at times we're too + our ailments continue where they do not belong!

2. Imagine being Peter's mother-in-law, so ill that you can hardly think or take your head off your pillow. Suddenly, Jesus says a few words over you and you feel as good as new. What would you say to him? Would your first thought be to get up and

serve? What do you think Luke meant to convey by including this detail?

Erei colmo di estasi e gratitude! ...mio Dio non mi hai abbandonato!

3. The sun was setting, and yet there were hordes of people clamoring around Jesus, waiting for healing. It had been a long day for him. What do you think was driving him to continue rather than just calling it a night?

Ha sentito la bona fame - e la Vanita compassione!

4. Why did Jesus cure people in Capernaum but not in his hometown of Nazareth (see Luke 4:23)? What was it about the atmosphere among the people in Capernaum that contributed to his desire to heal and bring about the reign of God?

Gente innocente e senza dubbi. Un profeta non mai conosciuto fra i suoi!

5. In Luke 4:43, Jesus says, "I must proclaim the good news of the kingdom of God to the other cities also; for I was sent for this purpose." What kind of kingdom did the Jewish people expect

the Messiah to inaugurate? Would this kingdom have a Messiah taking authority over evil spirits and illness?

un messia politico gesù non è avvenuto pei motivi politici

▶ In the Spotlight
Capernaum

Once Jesus launched his ministry, he moved to Capernaum, a fishing village on the northern shore of the Sea of Galilee, about two miles west of the Jordan River. It plays a large role in the Gospels; it is the place where Jesus called the fishermen Peter, Andrew, James, and John to follow him (Luke 5:1-11), as well as the tax collector Matthew (Matthew 9:9-13). All five men became his apostles.

Excavations at the site reveal a bustling town. At its center is a fourth-century synagogue, with some of its white limestone columns still standing. The synagogue was built on top of the one in which Jesus preached; the ruins of that structure, made of black basalt, can still be seen.

Also discovered is the house of Peter, the very one in which Jesus healed Peter's mother-in-law and in which the four men climbed on the roof to lower down the paralytic so that Jesus could heal their friend (Luke 5:17-26). The house is situated inside an octagonal church used by the early Christians. A modern church has been built over the site, enabling pilgrims to peer down into the ruins. As one gazes at Peter's house and the Sea of Galilee through the glass windows of the church, it's amazing to realize that Jesus really did live in this very same place.

Grow!

1. It is difficult to expect God to heal anyone if we do not have a sense that he is close at hand and invested in our lives and the lives of those around us. What signs do you see of God at work in your daily life? In the lives of people around you?

   _____

   _____

   _____

   _____

   _____

   _____

2. The New Testament is full of healing stories, and there is a long history of healing that continues to happen right down to the present day. Have you seen or heard about any instances of healing? What happened?

   _____

   _____

   _____

   _____

   _____

   _____

3. What do you expect to happen when you pray with someone directly or when you pray for them at Mass or during your daily prayer? Have you seen results that seem to be attributable to prayer? Share some examples.

   _____

   _____

   _____

   _____

4. It would seem that anyone who was actually healed by Jesus would want to follow him as a disciple. Some did, but many did not—even in Capernaum, the scene of this and many other miracles (see Matthew 11:23-24). In what ways have you experienced Jesus' healing touch? Did it make you more eager to follow him? Why or why not?

_____

_____

_____

_____

_____

_____

5. Luke's Gospel ends with Jesus' promise to the disciples that they would be "clothed with power from on high" (24:49). How did the release of the Holy Spirit in the lives of the disciples enable them to preach the gospel and heal? What are the implications of this for your life and faith?

_____

_____

_____

_____

_____

_____

Reflect!

In the Gospel of John, we read the powerful account of Jesus' last evening with his disciples before his crucifixion. A summation of the teaching Jesus has given them throughout his public ministry, this long discourse gives us a clear vision of the full life to which we are called. The call to servanthood, the call to love one another, the call to follow him in all things, the call to friendship with him, the call to unity—all of these invitations and more fill John 13–17.

Standing near the center of this body of teaching is this incredible declaration made by Jesus:

> "The one who believes in me will also do the works that I do and, in fact, will do greater works than these, because I am going to the Father. I will do whatever you ask in my name, so that the Father may be glorified in the Son. If in my name you ask me for anything, I will do it." (John 14:12-14)

Talk about expectations!

It would be easier for us if this passage were directed only at the apostles and their successors, but it is not. It is for all of us who believe in him.

Take time to think and pray about John 14:12-14. Ask the Lord to show you ways in which he desires you to "do the works" he has done. Review your life and activity in the light of John 13–17. Ask him what it might mean for you to do even "greater works," and pray for the faith to follow through with him.

Act!

Go to a friend or family member who is dealing with an illness or injury. Ask that person if he would let you pray with him for healing. If he agrees, invite him to join you in praying for faith and in rejecting doubt. Then pray with him on the spot for healing. Don't worry about what you see or don't see happen.

▶ In the Spotlight
An Epileptic Boy

I was visiting friends in a city far from home. One evening we got into an intense conversation about how we believed God was at work in our lives. I told them the story of my own healing, and one of them said, "You need to tell Ben that story." Ben was the eleven-year-old son of friends. He had been suffering from epilepsy for a number of years. To complicate the situation, he was also diagnosed as having an extreme hyperactivity disorder.

Ben was essentially a happy boy, but his medical problems were making his life difficult. Despite being on heavy medications for both of his conditions, he continued to have daily severe seizures at home and at school, and his hyperactivity was unchecked. Kids mocked him and bullied him.

Ben still had the simple faith of a child and was hoping against hope that God would do something to help him. My friends wanted him to hear my story because they believed that it might encourage him and give him even greater hope.

We got together with Ben and his parents and I told them my story, plus a few others about children I knew that had been healed. Ben was attentive throughout, in itself an unusual thing

for him. When I finished my stories, Ben asked if I would pray with him.

I told him that I would be glad to and asked what he wanted from the Lord. He said, "I have epilepsy really bad, and it makes life in school hard. The kids laugh at me and I just keep getting worse. I'm also really hyper, and that makes problems for me everywhere. Do you think Jesus can heal me?"

"Yes, Ben, I believe Jesus wants to heal you," were the words that came out of my mouth. I was surprised by my own sense of confidence, but I realized that I really wanted to see Ben healed and set free, and it was easy to believe that was exactly what the Lord wanted too.

We prayed simply and quietly. Ben closed his eyes and went completely silent. He was motionless for almost twenty-five minutes. His mother said he was not having a seizure, but everyone wondered if that was what was happening.

We uncomfortably went on talking and praying while Ben was there, apparently oblivious to all of us. Then he "woke up" and said, "Did you see what happened? It's like I couldn't move. It was okay, but I couldn't move, and then Jesus came and sat down beside me. He asked me what I wanted, and I told him everything, and he said he would do it for me."

I asked him if he had been healed, and he said, "No, no, I need you to pray with me again so that he can finish." I did, and the same thing happened, though not for as long a period of time. When Ben was "with us" again, he said, "He did it. Jesus healed me. He did it."

That night, his mother and father were astonished at how happy and calm Ben was. He did his homework, asked to go to bed a bit early, and the next day at school, his behavior had changed so completely that the school called his mother to ask if Ben was sick.

Ben never had another seizure, and his activity level toned down to that of a typical eleven-year-old boy. He asked his

doctor to help get him off of his drugs, and over a period of several months, the dosages were steadily reduced. The doctor was astonished. Previous attempts at even small reductions had always ended in disaster.

Finally, the doctor said, "Ben, you don't need to see me anymore. You have no signs of epilepsy and no signs of your hyperactivity disorder. I can't explain this. There isn't anything I've done that has helped you."

Ben said, "I can tell you what happened," and in his own wonderful way, he announced the good news of the kingdom of God. A new creation is being made, bit by bit, person by person. Ben is grown up now and still a friend of mine. He remains healthy.

I've often been struck by Ben's absolute innocence in asking for healing. It was a plea straight from the heart. His faith was neither mature nor well tested, but it was simple and pure. He expected God to do something, and that engendered a similar response in those of us who prayed with him. Praying for healing isn't about long, wordy prayers. It's about being in the presence of the Lord, asking him for what we need, and expecting him to act.

Waiting for
the Lord

John 5:2-9

[2] Now in Jerusalem by the Sheep Gate there is a pool, called in Hebrew Beth-zatha, which has five porticoes. [3] In these lay many invalids—blind, lame, and paralyzed. [5] One man was there who had been ill for thirty-eight years. [6] When Jesus saw him lying there and knew that he had been there a long time, he said to him, "Do you want to be made well?" [7] The sick man answered him, "Sir, I have no one to put me into the pool when the water is stirred up; and while I am making my way, someone else steps down ahead of me." [8] Jesus said to him, "Stand up, take your mat and walk." [9] At once the man was made well, and he took up his mat and began to walk.

The Pool of Beth-zatha (also known to us as the Pool of Bethesda or Bethsaida) near the Sheep Gate was a gathering spot for the sick and lame. From time to time, the waters of the pool would be disturbed, and whoever was first to get into the water at that moment would be healed of their sickness.

Let's imagine being there. The porticoes around the pool and the steps going down into the water are packed with people waiting for the moment when the waters will be stirred, and a palpable tension fills the air. No one knows when it will happen, and everyone wants to be the first in the pool. Many of the people have friends who are ready to help them into the pool, but there are also those who have no one to help them.

Such is the case of one man in particular. He has been waiting for God to heal him through the waters of this pool for thirty-eight years. Day after day, he is lying there on his crude bed with a mixed sense of hope and resignation. With his disability, the pool might as well

be miles away. The possibility of healing is so close at hand, and yet it seems impossibly distant and remote.

Jesus arrives. Instead of healing every person gathered around the pool, Jesus is drawn to the man who has been waiting there for so very, very long. His heart is moved by this patient, desperate faith.

Asking a man who has been ill for thirty-eight years whether he wants to be healed may seem like a very strange question, but living with unfulfilled hope does strange things to the mind and heart. Resignation can turn into doubt, doubt to disbelief, and disbelief can rob one of even the desire to be healed. So Jesus asks, "Do you want to be made well?" (John 5:6). The man's faith is still intact. He still patiently waits for what he believes God can do.

The man answers with an apologetic explanation of why he has not been healed. He has no idea what Jesus is ready to do for him. Jesus gives the man three simple commands: "Stand up, take up your mat and walk" (John 5:8). The man does as he is told.

Of course, if we read on in the story (John 5:10-18), we discover that the man almost instantly gets into trouble for carrying his mat on the Sabbath. He also gets persecuted for being healed on the Sabbath. Being healed does not necessarily mean stepping into a new life without any troubles!

Over the years, I have seen many instances of healing that happened instantly, at the very first moment of prayer. I have also seen many instances of healing that happened only after long periods of waiting and many experiences of prayer.

For the most part, we really don't know what is going to happen when we start praying for someone who is ill or when others pray for us in times of sickness. We don't know when Jesus is going to step into

the "portico" we are living in and ask us if we want to be healed. We live in a culture of instant gratification that demands results without delays, but that isn't the way things really work.

In 1995 I found out that the seemingly random illnesses I had experienced over the previous thirty years were all manifestations of one disease. I was diagnosed with Churg-Strauss syndrome and entered into a heavy regimen of oral chemotherapy drugs and thirty-one other medications. I had to quit work. My disease was considered to be incurable and terminal. Given the phase of the disease I was in, the doctors gave me two years or less to live.

In a matter of days, I had friends all over the country praying for me. My friends recruited their friends, and then people they didn't even know were praying for me. I would receive notes from convents and monasteries in faraway cities telling me that I was being remembered daily in their prayers.

I had experienced the healing power of God in my life before, but only in situations where my life was not at stake. I tried to wait for healing with patience, but my faith that God would actually heal me of this disease was on a very thin thread. I tried to prepare for death.

My symptoms multiplied, as did the barrage of prayers on my behalf. Numerous people would come and visit me and pray with me for healing, but gradually every major organ system in my body started to fail. My patience in waiting for healing gradually became impatience to have it all end. After many emergency-room visits and hospital stays, I ended up in coronary intensive care for what the doctors said were my final days.

On my second day there, a nurse's aide walked into my room and abruptly asked me if I had any fear. I was at peace about death, but the way I was dying was frightening. Ninety percent of my lung tissue

had been replaced by ineffective scar tissue. Every breath was a painful struggle. "Yes, I am afraid of the way I am dying," I told her.

The woman said, "Good. Jesus told me to come in here and tell you not to have any fear because he is here with you right now." I already believed he was there caring for me and "seeing me home," but as she spoke, I became aware of his presence in a completely different way.

"He also told me to tell you that starting right this moment, he is healing you. You need to be patient, because it is going to take some time. Just be faithful to him, because you *know* he is going to be faithful to you." With those words, she turned around and walked out of the room.

The next day the nephrologist told me that they were going to have to start kidney dialysis, as I had not had any kidney function at all for four days. Given my critical condition, dialysis was a great risk, but the toxins in my system were an even greater threat.

As he prepared my arm for a shunt, my kidneys suddenly started to function. He stopped the procedure in disbelief, but within twenty-four hours, he was able to declare that my kidneys were "perfect," after having declared them irreversibly dead only the day before.

Nine days later, my pulmonologist did a scan of my lungs because he could not understand how I had suddenly become able to breathe without any problem at all. He came to my room after studying the results, irate that he could not explain what he had seen. He said, "I've just looked at the most perfect lungs I have ever seen in my career." And so it went over the next several weeks. My failing heart that had been severely impaired, thickened, and enlarged suddenly became a "perfect" heart.

After a month of improvement, I still had many of my symptoms, and a group of my friends decided that enough was enough. My friend Paul said, "God has been healing Louie. Let's ask the Lord to finish the healing." They prayed with me for only a few seconds. There was a brilliant flash in my eyes that I could see, and Paul, who was in front of me, saw it as well. My cataracts disappeared. At the same instant, all of my other symptoms stopped, including my out-of-control diabetes.

The elastic bandages that were wrapped around my legs to control swelling became loose, and as I peeled them away, my friends were laughing and yelling, "Lazarus, come forth!" Visits to my medical doctors ended in tears. One said, "You are completely healed. This is not the result of medicine. Our treatments almost killed you. This is a great gift from God."

So when did my moment of healing really happen? Which of the numerous prayers on my behalf were the effective ones? Why did it take over thirty years of illness to get to this healing? Why did the healing take time and happen in stages?

The healing stories of Jesus do not give us many answers to such questions. While many of the cures that happen in the Gospel stories are instantaneous events, many of the people that are healed have been waiting a very long time for that moment, and some of the healings happen in short stages.

The story of the man at the pool for thirty-eight years may be an extreme case, but think of the stories of parents who have watched their children succumb to illness or death; think of the stories of people who have hoped and waited for God to intervene; think of the blind man who was first partially, then fully, healed (Mark 8:22-26); or of Lazarus, left to die from his sickness, then raised from the dead (John 11:1-44).

We always need to be ready to wait for the Lord. I think often of St. Monica waiting patiently year after year for her wayward son, St. Augustine, to turn around and follow the Lord. Were her prayers ineffective for all of those years? Hardly! In no small measure, they gave the Church two of its great saints, Monica herself, and Augustine.

Waiting for the Lord can purify our faith. The lack of an instant cure for our illnesses is no reason to stop praying for healing. There is always more to the picture than we can take in with a moment's glance.

Understand

1. The man in this story kept coming to the pool, even though he had no one to help him get to the water first. What do you think motivated him to keep going each day? What were his expectations?

_____

_____

_____

_____

_____

2. In so many other places, we see Jesus healing everyone who is brought to him or who comes to him. Here we see him seeking out one person. Why would Jesus walk into a place full of people waiting to be healed and single out this one man?

_____

_____

_____

_____

_____

3. Instead of saying yes when Jesus asks the man if he wants to be made well, the man tells Jesus why he hasn't yet been healed. What does this indicate about the man's state of mind? About his faith?

_____

_____

_____

_____

_____

_____

4. The man did not know who Jesus was (John 5:13). Why do you think he obeyed Jesus' command to stand up, take his mat, and walk? What if he had doubted?

_____

_____

_____

_____

_____

_____

5. Read the fuller story of the man at the pool from John 5:1-18. Jesus and the man he healed become the objects of persecution. The excuse of the Pharisees is that the healing is a violation of the sabbath laws, as was having the man carry his mat. What does Jesus see as the real issue?

_____

_____

_____

_____

▶ In the Spotlight
Jesus Did Not Heal Everyone

Jesus singles out the man at the Pool of Bethsaida for healing, even though there are many others lying there in need of healing. What are we to make of this? Here is what the *Catechism of the Catholic Church* tells us:

> Moved by so much suffering Christ not only allows himself to be touched by the sick, but he makes their miseries his own: "He took our infirmities and bore our diseases" (Matthew 8:17; cf. Isaiah 53:4). But he did not heal all the sick. His healings were signs of the coming of the Kingdom of God. They announced a more radical healing: the victory over sin and death through his Passover. On the cross Christ took upon himself the whole weight of evil and took away the "sin of the world" (John 1:29; cf. Isaiah 53:4-6), of which illness is only a consequence. By his passion and death on the cross Christ has given a new meaning to suffering: it can henceforth configure us to him and unite us with his redemptive Passion. (1505)

The *Catechism* also affirms that we won't all be healed, despite our prayers:

> The Holy Spirit gives to some a special charism of healing so as to make manifest the power of the grace of the risen Lord. But even the most intense prayers do not always obtain the healing of all illnesses. Thus St. Paul must learn from the Lord that "my grace is sufficient for you, for my power is made perfect in weakness" (2 Corinthians 12:9), and that the sufferings to be endured can mean that "in my flesh I complete what is lacking in

Christ's afflictions for the sake of his Body, that is, the Church" (Colossians 1:24). (1508)

Grow!

1. What do you find most difficult about waiting for the Lord to act? What has most helped you to wait with hope and expectant faith?

_____

_____

_____

_____

_____

_____

2. Recall a time when you repeatedly asked the Lord for something. Did you have to wait a long time for an answer? Are you still waiting? If so, do you believe you will eventually get an answer, even if it's not the answer you want?

_____

_____

_____

_____

_____

_____

3. Waiting can sometimes cause us to question what we think we want or need. Recall a time when God used a situation in which you had to wait to change your desire for something. Did you get something better than what you had asked for?

_____

_____

_____

_____

_____

_____

4. Jesus cured a woman who had been bent over for eighteen years, also on the Sabbath, and he was also criticized for it (Luke 13:10-17). From this episode, what can you say about how Jesus looks at waiting?

_____

_____

_____

_____

_____

5. Patience is a hard-won gift—one that we should only ask for carefully—but it is a gift indeed! Are you going through any situation right now that calls for patience? How might prayer asking for this gift help you? How might Jesus be already answering you?

_____

_____

_____

_____

Reflect!

Spend time with Jesus at the pool of Bethsaida. Ask him to help you see what he is seeing. This is a place of great suffering and also of great hope. Look at the man who has been waiting for thirty-eight years. What is in Jesus' heart and mind as he looks at the man? Go through the entire scene with Jesus. Then go through the scene

with the man as well. Imagine what is going through his mind, and imagine what he must feel when Jesus heals him. The man's patience has been rewarded in a completely unexpected way. Ask that, more and more, you would have the mind and heart of Jesus toward every person you meet, along with his patience.

Act!

Think carefully about what is going on in your life right now. Is there any specific area where you are finding it extremely difficult to find patience, either with yourself or with someone else? Ask the Lord to help you develop a strategy for dealing with the situation in a practical way. What things can you do or say or hear that will help you short-circuit impatience and be more open to the way the Lord wants to work in the situation?

▶ In the Spotlight
Living with Pain and Suffering

Even casual reading of the lives of the saints reveals a frequent theme that may not appeal to us very much. We look at the Little Flower, St. Thérèse of the Child Jesus, and see a sweet young woman suffering a long illness that leads to her death. St. Bernadette Soubirous followed a similar path.

St. Ignatius of Loyola was so hard on his body when he first came to know the Lord that he was afflicted in his later years with constant stomach pain. And the world watched Pope St. John Paul II slowly succumb to Parkinson's disease.

Of course, there are also the stories of the martyrs and the sufferings they endured. Paul's letters and the Acts of the Apostles are filled with stories of pain inflicted by others and

of good disciples dealing with illnesses, from the near-fatal sickness of Epaphroditus recounted in Philippians 2:25-30 to Paul's own torments.

Jesus does not promise us that our lives will be without suffering. The new heaven and new earth are on their way, slowly unfolding before us, but they have not fully arrived. Until they do, sickness, suffering, pain, and death are a part of life.

How do men and women of God deal with suffering and pain? Do we follow the pattern of the world and react in fear and dread? Do we give in to self-pity, depression, and anger at our miserable lot in life? Do we hide our pain or, conversely, wear it on our sleeves and in every word we say? Do we become constant complainers or strike out at others as though they were the cause of our pain?

When we look at Jesus in his passion and death, we first see that he shares the same dread of suffering that we do. The scene of Jesus in the Garden of Gethsemane is about as raw and real as it gets. In Matthew's account, Jesus throws himself on the ground and prays three times to his Father to "let this cup pass from me" (26:39-44). In Mark's Gospel, we see the exact same scene with the added information that Jesus is agitated (14:33-34). In Luke, we see that in Jesus' tormented prayer, his sweat becomes like "great drops of blood falling down on the ground" (22:44).

This is a fully human reaction to the torture, pain, and death that Jesus understands he is facing at this point. There is no blithe run to embrace what is dreadful to all of us who are made of flesh and blood. It is human and very normal to experience fear in the face of pain and suffering.

But Jesus does not stay locked in his dread. He reaches out of his fear for the touch of his Father. He asks for relief and, yes, even asks for escape, but then he sets his own yearning aside and bends his own will to the will of his Father: "Not my will but yours be done" (Luke 22:42).

As simple as this response seems, there are many layers to it. First, there is Jesus' recognition that in his humanity, accepting the coming torment is not something he can do alone. He asks his Father for relief.

Second, his request for relief is conditioned by his greater desire to fulfill the will of his Father. No matter how much he may fear what is coming upon him, Jesus' love for his Father and for all the Father is doing in this turning point of history takes priority.

Third, it is essential that Jesus voice his fear. It is a declaration of his embrace of his full humanity, but it also shows a recognition that humans can't fully deal with things they hide or don't acknowledge. Jesus cannot overcome his fear by pretending it is not there or by somehow denying its existence.

Fourth, once Jesus has laid out everything on the table with his Father, he knows it is time to move forward. He knew long ago that torment and death were a necessary part of the path he was walking. That does not stop him from having fear or dread about it all, but having acknowledged those very real emotions, he is ready to face it head-on.

So what does this tell us about dealing with pain and suffering in our own lives?

First, we are not capable of handling pain on our own. We cannot bear the weight of suffering if we choose to stand alone. There is an irony in this, as pain and suffering can tend to be isolating experiences. In the midst of great pain, be it physical or emotional, we tend to feel that we really are alone.

Yet Jesus himself has been in this moment, as have hundreds of millions of others through the ages, as well as many of our own friends and family members. We need the same support and relief that Jesus sought from his disciples and from his Father. It is there for the asking. Simply acknowledging that we cannot do it on our own breaks down the walls of our isolation.

Second, as much as we like to think that we are in control of our lives and our circumstances, we are not. We *are* in control of the decisions and choices that we make, but our decisions and choices encounter the decisions and choices of others and the circumstances of our physical world. We don't control outcomes, only our choices.

Like Jesus, we seek to align our choices and decisions with the will of God as well as we can know it. Discernment will lead us to an understanding of his will for us in this moment, and it may not always match up with what we might be more inclined to do. Like Jesus in the garden, it is right and good for us to express to the Lord what our desire or inclination is in the situation, but then we need to take it another step and join him in saying, "Not my will but yours be done."

Third, like Jesus, if we recognize that God is asking us to walk through something very difficult and painful, it is right and good for us to acknowledge our fear and to surrender that to the Lord.

Finally, when we have surrendered our self-sufficiency, when we have let go of our need to control every outcome, and when we have surrendered our fears, Jesus shows us the next step: simply pressing on with the life we are called to live, no matter what its limits or challenges may be.

That life may be riddled with pain and struggle, but that is no more than what our master endured before us. As Paul says, we make up in our own suffering what is incomplete in the suffering of Jesus (Colossians 1:24). In the mystery of our union with Jesus, we become participants in his suffering in a tangible way.

We participate in the work of bringing God's new heaven and new earth into being in the same way that Jesus did and that he continues to do in his mystical body. If we will allow it, his presence in us and with us transforms our pain into his own.

We know that his suffering is winning that victory for all of his children, and we are a part of that work. Living with pain is not easy. Following Jesus as his disciple is not easy, but we know that it ultimately leads to resurrection.

Pain is not to be feared.

Faith, Wherever It Can Be Found

Mark 2:1-12

When he returned to Capernaum after some days, it was reported that he was at home. [2] So many gathered around that there was no longer room for them, not even in front of the door; and he was speaking the word to them. [3] Then some people came, bringing to him a paralyzed man, carried by four of them. [4] And when they could not bring him to Jesus because of the crowd, they removed the roof above him; and after having dug through it, they let down the mat on which the paralytic lay. [5] When Jesus saw their faith, he said to the paralytic, "Son, your sins are forgiven." [6] Now some of the scribes were sitting there, questioning in their hearts, [7] "Why does this fellow speak in this way? It is blasphemy! Who can forgive sins but God alone?" [8] At once Jesus perceived in his spirit that they were discussing these questions among themselves; and he said to them, "Why do you raise such questions in your hearts? [9] Which is easier, to say to the paralytic, 'Your sins are forgiven,' or to say, 'Stand up and take your mat and walk'? [10] But so that you may know that the Son of Man has authority on earth to forgive sins"—he said to the paralytic— [11] "I say to you, stand up, take your mat and go to your home." [12] And he stood up, and immediately took the mat and went out before all of them; so that they were all amazed and glorified God, saying, "We have never seen anything like this!"

Jesus has just returned from a mission trip to the towns of Galilee. Now he is at Peter's house, teaching the visitors who have squeezed inside. There is no room to move. The dust of shuffling feet hangs in the air. The crowd is backed up out the door and into the street. It is a crowd of people hungry to hear more of what Jesus has to say, people waiting to see if he will heal anyone, people who are merely curious, and people waiting to trap him in some statement that would show him to be a fraud. It is not an easy audience.

At the back of the crowd, there is a ruckus as four people carry a paralyzed man on a mat through the streets. Those that block their path and the door are too interested in hearing what Jesus is saying to make way for them. Frustrated, the four look for other options.

With a fresh idea, they climb up onto the roof of the house and begin to dismantle it. In the house, there is a sudden shower of dust, dried clay, and wood. In moments there is a huge hole in the ceiling, and sunlight streams in, putting Jesus in a spotlight.

Suspended by ropes, the mat carrying the paralytic slowly descends to a spot cleared of people by the fallen debris. Jesus can't help but smile. Such faith! This poor man is rich in friends. With great affection, Jesus says, "Son, your sins are forgiven" (Mark 2:5).

His sins are forgiven? That's not what the man or his friends are expecting, and it's a shock for the scribes who are present. Their minds start racing. "How can he forgive sins? This man is a blasphemer. He is doing what only God can do."

Jesus knows their reaction, and he confronts them with a question they will not answer. "Which is easier—forgiving sin or healing the man?" (cf. Mark 2:9). He turns to the paralytic and says, "Stand up, take your mat and go to your home" (2:11). Without a word, the man stands. There is a gasp of wonder throughout the entire room. The men on the roof are jubilant.

The man takes his mat, finds his way through the crowd, and heads for home. His friends scurry down to embrace him. They are oblivious to the mess they have left behind. How can they think of anything other than this healing?

In the house and in the street, the crowd erupts in a giddy buzz of conversation and exclamation. "Have you ever seen anything like this?"

It is clear that if one is going to ask Jesus for healing, faith is central to the request. But in the stories of healing that we read in the Gospels and Acts, it is not always clear which person has to have that faith. Is it the person who needs healing, as we see in Mark 10:46-52? Is it a friend or family member, as in Mark 2:1-5? When we see the apostles and disciples healing people, is it because of their faith (Acts 3:2-8) or because of the faith of those who come to them (5:14-16)?

Surprisingly, there is not one answer. In the case of the paralytic, nothing at all is said about the man's faith. Instead, the text seems to indicate that Jesus sees the faith of the man's friends and responds to that. There are numerous accounts of people bringing the sick to Jesus, and they are all healed.

For the man at the pool (John 5:2-9), his faith is not in Jesus. He doesn't even know who Jesus is, but he knows that healing happens at the pool. Jesus heals him because the man believes that God will heal him.

In the story of the woman with the hemorrhage (Mark 5:25-34) and in many other stories, people come to Jesus to be healed because they believe he can do it, even if all they do is touch his robe.

Faith is essential, but where that faith is lodged may not be so important. It does not have to be found in the person that needs the healing. It does not have to be found in each one of their friends or family members. Jesus says that it only takes faith the size of a mustard seed to pray with power (Matthew 17:20).

Sometimes when we pray for someone who is seriously ill, it can seem hard to find faith the size of an atom, much less a mustard seed. It takes more than a raw belief that healing is something that God can do "in principle." When we see people coming to Jesus for healing,

they or their friends or family come with a passionate conviction that not only can Jesus heal but that *he will*.

When I first met someone who had been physically healed of a serious illness, I was in awe. I was certain that they must be exceptionally holy, exceptionally close to the Lord. They must have "earned" their healing.

But like everything else in a relationship with the Lord, "earning" is not a part of the picture. Over time, I met people who were, in their own words, "deeply flawed" and yet had been healed when someone had prayed with them. All of them had a realistic sense of having been "unworthy" to be healed, but they also carried an understanding of how freely they were loved by the Lord.

I also discovered that their being healed did not produce instant perfection in other areas of their lives. If they were struggling with certain issues before they were healed, they were likely to continue to struggle with those same issues after they were healed. Often they had greater faith and confidence in the Lord, and so they were able to confront these struggles with a deeper understanding of the Lord's mercy and forgiveness.

Jesus frequently gave forgiveness before he even gave healing, not because the person's sins were the cause of their particular illness, but because that is what we all need the most. We are sinners. Sickness is in the world because of sin, not our sins in particular, but the sins of all humanity, the sin of Adam.

Faith in the power of God to heal when we pray with others or when we are prayed with is something that grows. The more people I came to know who had been healed and the more I read the stories of others, the more my own faith grew.

When I first stepped out and prayed with someone for healing, I expected very little to happen. I thought that perhaps the person would "feel closer to the Lord." I think I was praying for someone with a bad headache. Imagine my surprise when they told me that the headache was instantly gone!

I made many more "attempts," with more failures than successes, but I kept on trying. A dramatic healing of my lower back upped the ante, and for a time I was able to pray with even more faith, with good results.

I began to realize that faith needs to be exercised and fed to grow and become strong. When I was healed of Churg-Strauss disease, my perspective was then altered radically. I had been literally brought back from my deathbed.

Not long after I was healed, I ran into the archbishop of our diocese. He had heard about my healing, and he embraced me with excitement and said, "You have to tell people what God is doing. He is still at work in power. Tell everyone you can. People need to hear that!"

One of the best ways to make a small fire of faith grow is to fan it. People with whom I shared my story found new courage to go and pray with sick and injured friends, not because of me, but because of what God had done. People want to know that the new creation really is coming, that the power of the Holy Spirit in us is real, and that Jesus cares about what is happening here and now.

Ultimately, our faith is not in the power of God to heal. Our faith is in God's love and in his intention, desire, and will to gather all things together in Christ, to bring us to that day when there will be no more tears, when sickness and even death will no longer be

our lot. Healing at the hands of the Lord merely underscores the direction in which he is moving all of creation.

Let's fan the flame!

Understand

1. In this passage, it is clear that Jesus is already a "celebrity." People hear that he is in town and rush to see him. What do you think they were looking to find? What might have been their expectations? What were the expectations of the four friends?

_____

_____

_____

_____

_____

2. Imagine being in the house with Jesus and then hearing and seeing the hole being made in the roof above you. Would you be annoyed or angry about the disturbance? What was Jesus' reaction?

_____

_____

_____

_____

_____

3. Why did Jesus first tell the paralyzed man that his sins were forgiven? What might have been the man's reaction to such a statement? Do you think he was even aware that he needed to be forgiven?

_____

_____

_____

_____

_____

_____

4. The scribes believed that only God had the power and right to forgive sin, so Jesus' first remark to the paralytic was bound to cause a stir. What does Jesus' answer to their concern mean? What do you think the scribes thought after they saw Jesus heal the man?

_____

_____

_____

_____

_____

_____

5. Jesus used this healing to show that he had the authority on earth to forgive sins. Do you think that witnessing such a dramatic healing would have changed the way the people viewed Jesus? How did the crowd respond?

_____

_____

_____

_____

_____

_____

▶ In the Spotlight
Jesus' Authority

"Who can forgive sins but God alone?" That's the question posed to Jesus by the scribes (Mark 2:7). The Father has given Jesus the authority to forgive sins, and Jesus demonstrates that truth by healing the paralytic. Yet this passage from Mark is just the beginning of a series of episodes in which Jesus' authority will be questioned, leading eventually to his passion and death.

In his *Dictionary of Biblical Theology*, Fr. Xavier Léon-Dufour notes that during his public life, "Jesus appears as the recipient of a singular authority (*exousia*)":

> He preaches to remit sin (Matthew 9:6), and he is Lord of the Sabbath (Mark 2:28). He has all the spiritual power of a divine envoy before whom the Jews pose the essential question: by what authority does he do these things (Matthew 21:23)? Jesus does not respond directly to this question (Matthew 21:27). But the signs that he accomplishes sharpen their thoughts to an answer: he has power (*exousia*) over sickness (Matthew 8:8), over the elements (Mark 4:41), and over demons (Matthew 12:28). His authority, then, extends even to political things; in this domain, the power which he refused to take from Satan (Luke 4:5) he has received in reality from God.

We would not expect someone with this power and authority, however, to act like Jesus:

> He does not take advantage of this power among men. At the time when the leaders of this world manifest it to them by exercising dominion, he displays himself among his own as the one who serves (Luke 22:25). He is master and Lord (John 13:13); but he has come to serve and

to give his life (Mark 10:42). And it is because he takes on the condition of a slave that all knees will eventually bend before him (Philippians 2:5-11). That is why, after his resurrection, he will tell his followers that from then on "all power (*exousia*) has been given him in heaven and on earth" (Matthew 28:18).

Grow!

1. When we hear faith spoken of in the Gospels, it is almost always something that can be seen as well as heard. Real faith moves people to act: to reach out to touch Jesus, to make a request of him, to call out to him over the din of a crowd, or to get out of a boat and walk on the water. It may be fragile, but it brings about action. Think of a recent time when you demonstrated such faith. What happened?

_____

_____

_____

_____

_____

_____

2. The four friends of the paralyzed man were both bold and creative. How do these two qualities help us to act on what we believe?

_____

_____

_____

_____

_____

_____

3. How does your faith affect the way you relate to and treat other people? What difference does it make?

_____

_____

_____

_____

_____

_____

4. Has your love for someone ever empowered you to step out and exercise your faith on their behalf? If so, what happened? If not, what held you back?

_____

_____

_____

_____

_____

_____

5. Think about the day or the week ahead of you. Are there situations that you know may come up in which you would have an opportunity to act on your faith in Jesus? (The operative word here is "act," which may involve speaking, but may not.) Name those opportunities and make a plan for responding to them.

_____

_____

_____

_____

_____

_____

Reflect!

Reflect on the combination of faith and love that led the four men to bring their paralytic friend to Jesus, even though it meant taking the roof off a house. Love can lead us to do many extraordinary things. Faith can do likewise. Combined, they are an unstoppable power.

As we relate to Jesus, we grow in faith and love. We experience his love for us, and that love cannot help but overflow to others. The deepest love has its source in Jesus. The best friendships and relationships find their strength in Jesus. The power to love those who might be difficult for us to love comes from Jesus.

Reflect on the faith of the four men and on your own faith. How close to Jesus are you willing to let faith take you? How much love are you willing to give him? How much love do you freely accept from him? Do you hold back or keep a part of your life or heart for yourself alone?

Say that simple prayer that comes right out of the Gospels to help us: "I believe; help my unbelief" (Mark 9:24). Let the embers of your faith grow into a spreading fire of love.

Act!

Make a decision to spend time every day in conversation with Jesus, not just telling him things you want to say, but also listening to him. Take the Gospels into your prayer time, and let him speak to you through them. Ask for help in hearing him speak to your mind and heart. Daily ask for more faith and love. Ask to have your life overflow with the love and power of his Holy Spirit.

▶ In the Spotlight
A Few Good Friends

Tim was a successful surgeon, known and recognized throughout the small city where he lived. Highly trusted as a doctor, he made it a point of getting to know his patients and of letting them get to know him so that they could go into surgery with greater confidence. He was also known as a man of great faith who had come to the Church as an adult. He was a leader in his parish, generous to various charities with his money, time, and skills, and the kind of affable person that makes you feel happy just to see him.

One day as he was preparing to go into surgery, he suddenly found his vision blurred. He washed his eyes out and the sensation passed; but in the coming weeks the blurriness returned repeatedly, sometimes for only a moment and sometimes for longer periods of time.

More alarmingly, Tim began to experience weakness in his hands that again would come and go without warning. He began to dread the possibility of being in surgery and having either the blurred vision or weakness happen while he was operating on someone.

He went to see his own doctor, and after a very long process of testing and evaluation, he received his diagnosis. He had myasthenia gravis, a rare autoimmune disorder that causes muscle weakness, frequently manifesting itself in the muscles of the face and particularly of the eyes. The disease is progressive and incurable.

Tim was devastated. He closed his surgical practice and limited himself to consulting. In his depression, he found himself angry at God and withdrew from his parish. The affability that had marked his relationships disappeared. He became an angry, bitter man, increasingly turned in on himself.

His friends and patients were all deeply saddened by what they saw, both in terms of his illness and in terms of the direction

of his life. People continually tried to reach out to him, but they were always rebuffed, sometimes harshly and sometimes with deep sadness.

Some of his friends heard that there was going to be a healing rally in their city, and they decided that they wanted to get Tim to go. It seemed improbable that he would have any interest in such an event, but over the next few weeks, he was invited again and again.

The event was going to be presented on four evenings. "You don't need to go to all of them. Just come once!" Tim's friends would say. He turned them down but with less vehemence than he had before. His disease was leaving him weaker and unable to fight anything.

The rally began on a Tuesday evening, and many people in the room were watching the doors for Tim to show up. They waited again on Wednesday and Thursday. Finally, on Friday evening, a buzz of excitement went through the crowd: "Dr. Tim is here!"

Tim, however, was not excited. He came because he didn't want people hounding him about why he hadn't show up. He came because he was tired. He came because he didn't know what else to do.

That evening one of the speakers told a personal story about being healed of a rare autoimmune disorder. Tim knew much more than he cared to about autoimmune disorders, and he knew well the disease the speaker was describing. It was in the same family of disorders as myasthenia gravis, and it was also an incurable, terminal disease with horrible side effects.

Soon Tim was completely caught up in the story of the man's sickness and then of his healing. His eyes were nearly popping out of his head, and when the time came for people at the rally to be prayed with, the speaker walked right over to Tim and asked him if he was ready. Tim said yes.

A small group of his friends gathered around him, and they all prayed that God would heal Tim right then and there. The prayer lasted all of thirty seconds, and suddenly, Tim, who was sitting in the middle of the group, leaped up and yelled at the top of his lungs, "Oh my God, I've been healed! I've been healed!"

Everyone in the room heard his yell, and everyone believed him. The place erupted in applause, shouts of thanks to God, and singing. Tim was so excited that he could hardly contain himself. He said to those around him, "Every symptom is gone. I feel great. Look at my hands. Look at me jumping. I can see clearly. God is so good! Thank you. Thank you, Jesus."

Tim had not wanted to go to the rally. Even when he finally gave in to his friends, he remained reluctant. His body language through the first part of the gathering was that of an angry skeptic enduring some kind of punishment. But he never would have been there if his friends had not continued their gentle urging and literally brought him through the door. He could have remained in his sickness and bitterness, but a few good friends saved him from himself.

Faith is critical, but in the end, it is all about love.

Who Is Worthy?

Luke 7:1-10

[1]After Jesus had finished all his sayings in the hearing of the people, he entered Capernaum. [2]A centurion there had a slave whom he valued highly, and who was ill and close to death. [3]When he heard about Jesus, he sent some Jewish elders to him, asking him to come and heal his slave. [4]When they came to Jesus, they appealed to him earnestly, saying, "He is worthy of having you do this for him, [5]for he loves our people, and it is he who built our synagogue for us." [6]And Jesus went with them, but when he was not far from the house, the centurion sent friends to say to him, "Lord, do not trouble yourself, for I am not worthy to have you come under my roof; [7]therefore I did not presume to come to you. But only speak the word, and let my servant be healed. [8]For I also am a man set under authority, with soldiers under me; and I say to one, 'Go,' and he goes, and to another, 'Come,' and he comes, and to my slave, 'Do this,' and the slave does it." [9]When Jesus heard this he was amazed at him, and turning to the crowd that followed him, he said, "I tell you, not even in Israel have I found such faith." [10]When those who had been sent returned to the house, they found the slave in good health.

Capernaum is a fortunate town. Rome is an oppressor. The Roman military presence is an ongoing reminder that the hopes of the Jewish people remain unfulfilled, but here in this town that often hosts Jesus, there is an exception to the rule. A Roman centurion who is respected and even honored by the people keeps watch over the town. He is a good man. He has done nothing but show respect and care for the people who live there. He has even built the synagogue where Jesus often teaches.

An important member of the centurion's household has fallen critically ill. Rather than trouble Jesus and create a public scene, he begs some of the elders of the town to ask Jesus to heal his servant. So they make the request.

Impressed that this Roman would ask for the help of a Jewish teacher, Jesus heads for the centurion's home at once. Before they even arrive, friends of the centurion bring a message. "Don't trouble yourself, Lord. I am not worthy that you should come under my roof" (cf. Luke 7:6). The Roman knows that his home is not considered "clean" under Jewish law.

But the centurion's message continues. He understands something about Jesus that few others do. He sees the unique authority that Jesus has. He knows that authority can be delegated. Jesus only needs to speak the word, and the healing will happen. There is no need for Jesus to be present.

Jesus is struck with both joy and pain: joy at the faith of this Roman and pain at the fact that there isn't faith anything like it in all of Israel. Jesus does not even have to utter any words of healing. His acknowledgment of the centurion's faith is enough. The slave is cured.

I have always loved this story. Here is a man who, under Jewish law, is an outsider. He is not one of the chosen. Even Jesus would say that he has been sent to the house of Israel (Matthew 15:24) and not to the Romans or others, but here is a representative of the "divine" Caesar with life-changing faith, not in the emperor, but in Jesus.

Jesus can't hold back what the man asks for. Undoubtedly, if the centurion had come to Jesus to express his gratitude, Jesus would have said, "Your faith has saved your servant."

Jesus' love easily bridges whatever religious, political, or social gap there might be. He shows mercy to the centurion and to tax collectors, who were often (accurately) perceived as thieves. He brings mercy and forgiveness to prostitutes, and he frees those beset by demons. His love is without boundaries.

When it comes to healing, there is no qualification list for who might be healed. That means that you and I are "eligible" to be healed, and so is anyone that we might come across who is in need of healing. We don't need to go through a "worthiness checklist" to see whether it is acceptable to pray with that person. And we don't need to go through such a checklist for ourselves. If the worry is about your own worthiness, admit that you are a sinner—you are on the same footing as all the rest of us!

Very often, it is easier to give than to receive. Praying with others for healing can actually be a very joyful and hope-filled experience. Having others pray with us can be more of a challenge.

For me, the experience of being prayed with literally hundreds of times by many hundreds of people over the years has been a personal journey into unfamiliar areas of humility. I learned a long time ago that there is not much room for pride in a hospital bed. If you spend enough time as a patient, no body part goes unexposed, unprodded, or unevaluated. You either get over the embarrassment or you make yourself unnecessarily uncomfortable. So after all of that, it's still a mystery to me why my asking for prayers from friends and well-wishers should still be a challenge. But it often has been.

The problem often comes down to one of feeling unworthy. "I love attention, so therefore I am unworthy of the attention of people praying for me." "I'm a miserable sinner. I can't be worthy of healing." "I'm too proud. God would never want to work through me to heal

someone else!" 5"I don't even like this person. I can't be worthy of praying with them."

There is an antidote to feeling unworthy: humility. Yes, you may be unworthy by all kinds of standards that you can construct for yourself, but by the standard of the living God, worthiness does not enter the picture. The centurion could not have been much more unworthy under the Jewish law, but he accepted that fact in humility and begged through intermediaries that Jesus would heal his honored slave.

You are a son or daughter of an infinitely loving God. You don't need any other qualification to receive his love or to be healed. You don't need any other qualification to exercise your freedom to pray for the healing of others. Humility serves those praying as well as those being prayed with.

As the kingdom of God continues to be revealed, Jesus invites us to work side by side with him in extending it. He invites us to manifest the signs of the coming new creation, and he alone is our worthiness. There is no need to hold back.

Understand

1. The Roman centurion had "heard about Jesus" (Luke 7:3). What do you think caused him to be so sure that Jesus could heal his servant?

_____

_____

_____

_____

_____

2. Why do you think the centurion had such a great respect for the Jews and their religion? What kind of relationship do you think he had with the Jewish elders, on whom he relied to carry his message to Jesus?

_____

_____

_____

_____

_____

3. Why did Jesus respond so readily and agree to come to the centurion's house? Do you think he was moved by the Jewish elders' description of him?

_____

_____

_____

_____

_____

4. What was the centurion's understanding of authority? How did this compare to Jesus' understanding?

_____

_____

_____

_____

_____

5. We repeat the words of the centurion at every Mass: "Lord, I am not worthy that you should enter under my roof, but only say the word and my soul shall be healed." What does this prayer mean to you? Why did the Church choose it for the liturgy?

_____

_____

_____

_____

_____

_____

▶ In the Spotlight
The Roman Centurion

Centurions play key roles in the New Testament and are uniformly spoken of favorably. In addition to this story, there is the centurion who, at Jesus' crucifixion, states, "Truly this man was God's Son!" (Matthew 27:54). In the Acts of the Apostles, Peter, after a vision from God, is sent to the house of Cornelius, "a centurion of the Italian Cohort" (10:1). Cornelius is described as "a devout man who feared God with all his household; he gave alms generously to the people and prayed constantly to God" (10:2). He and his household are the first Gentiles to receive the Holy Spirit and are subsequently baptized (10:44-48). Finally, the centurion Julius saves Paul's life when he is in danger of being thrown overboard by soldiers (27:39-44).

A centurion was the commander of one hundred men (although the number often varied) in a Roman legion of 6,000. Centurions were the backbone of the Roman army, working their way up the ranks as soldiers and promoted for their dedication and courage. The treatise *De Re Militari* (*Concerning Military Matters*) written by Vegetius, a Latin writer of the later Roman Empire, wrote this about the qualities necessary in a centurion:

The centurion in the infantry is chosen for his size, strength and dexterity in throwing his missile weapons and for his skill in the use of his sword and shield; in short for his expertness in all the exercises. He is to be vigilant, temperate, active and readier to execute the orders he receives than to talk; strict in exercising and keeping up proper discipline among his soldiers, in obliging them to appear clean and well-dressed and to have their arms constantly rubbed and bright.

Grow!

1. In your relationship with the Lord, do you ever struggle with a sense of unworthiness? How does this manifest itself? How do you deal with it?

_____
_____
_____
_____
_____
_____

2. Do you ever find yourself wrestling with your perception of whether other people are worthy—worthy of some honor, worthy of love, worthy of some blessing or grace? What impact does this have on the way you relate to them?

_____
_____
_____
_____
_____
_____

3. Who is an "outsider" to you? Perhaps it is someone you know who is not a believer or who is from another culture. In what ways might Jesus be calling you to reach out to that person?

_____

_____

_____

_____

_____

4. Have you ever felt unworthy to pray with someone else for healing? To be prayed with for healing? If so, what might the Lord say to you about this?

_____

_____

_____

_____

_____

5. How can the admission that you are a sinner help you to be bolder in your faith? How might it help you to see others?

_____

_____

_____

_____

_____

Reflect!

Spend some quiet time with the Lord. In a notebook or journal, write down times in your life when you could see that he was showing you his love. Include times in your life that have been filled with goodness and joy. Think back to times of joy in your relationships or moments of experiencing the beauty of his creation—any kind of moment that is marked by love, joy, or peace. Ask the Lord to help you see moments that you might not remember. Write until you can't think of any more such moments, and then take time to give thanks to the Lord for always seeing you as one he loves.

Take a little more time to give thanks for each of the people in your life, no matter what the relationship is or how the relationship stands at the moment.

Act!

In your notebook, following the things you have given thanks for, begin a list of stories you have heard about people being healed. These can be stories that you have heard directly from the person healed, stories that other people have told you, stories you have read, and so forth. You don't need to write out the whole story. Just put down enough words to remind you of the essentials.

▶ In the Spotlight
The Hemorrhaging Woman

Read Mark 5:25-34 and consider the following modern-day true story.

Ellen attended a healing service at church. She did not go there expecting anything to happen. She had a chronic physical problem; she was bleeding all of the time. She had been to numerous doctors and clinics and had tried many treatments and medications, but nothing resolved her problem for more than a day or two. Of course, her problem was hardly the kind of thing one would bring up in conversation, and so she did not ask anyone beyond her husband to pray for her.

Ellen attended the healing service more out of curiosity than anything else. She knew several people with health issues who planned to be there, and she was hoping that something might happen for them.

That night the leader of the service built his preaching around a particular story from Scripture—the story from Mark of the woman suffering with a chronic hemorrhage.

Ellen was stunned. She turned red, feeling as though everyone in the church was looking at her. Of course they were not, but as the speaker continued to share, she felt as if her life story were being told. She suddenly realized that she *did* want to be healed.

When the time came for people to be prayed with, Ellen quickly scanned the lineup of people who were praying with others. She didn't know any of them except for one. That was a relief. She wasn't going to have to reveal her problem to a friend.

She made her way to one of the other team members, but the waiting line was interminable. In fact, the lines were long for every single team member but the one she knew, and he was motioning her to come up and get prayed with.

Ellen swallowed hard and walked up to Bill and hesitantly told him her story. "This has been going on for years, Bill, and

I've never asked anyone else to pray for me." Bill said, "I think the Lord wants to heal you." Ellen replied, "I think so too."

Bill only had to pray with Ellen very briefly and simply. As he did, Ellen felt a change in her body. She looked up at Bill and said, "It's happened. I know I'm healed!" Her problem had ended once and for all. Later, a routine visit to her medical clinic produced an astounded reaction from her doctor, who was dumbfounded. Nothing she or the other doctors had tried had ever helped, and now Ellen was completely well.

Later, Ellen was rummaging through an old diary, and she came across the entry from the day her problem began. It was exactly twelve years to the day before she had been healed. She quickly opened her Bible to the passage in Mark about the woman healed of a bleeding problem. She read, "Now there was a woman who had been suffering from hemorrhages for twelve years" (5:25). Ellen wept tears of thanksgiving.

God's mercy and healing are given freely to those who come to him in humility and trust. Shame and embarrassment and a peculiar sense of unworthiness had prevented Ellen from asking even her closest friends for prayer. But she was attentive to God's word, and when she heard the Gospel story, her heart was opened and she readily sought his healing love in deep humility.

When There Is No Healing

Matthew 17:14-20

¹⁴ When they came to the crowd, a man came to him, knelt before him, ¹⁵ and said, "Lord, have mercy on my son, for he is an epileptic and he suffers terribly; he often falls into the fire and often into the water. ¹⁶ And I brought him to your disciples, but they could not cure him." ¹⁷ Jesus answered, "You faithless and perverse generation, how much longer must I be with you? How much longer must I put up with you? Bring him here to me." ¹⁸ And Jesus rebuked the demon, and it came out of him, and the boy was cured instantly. ¹⁹ Then the disciples came to Jesus privately and said, "Why could we not cast it out?" ²⁰ He said to them, "Because of your little faith. For truly I tell you, if you have faith the size of a mustard seed, you will say to this mountain, 'Move from here to there,' and it will move; and nothing will be impossible for you."

The disciples have been announcing the good news and accompanying it with signs and wonders. They, too, have become healers, but they are still learning and uncertain about the gifts that Jesus has given them.

As Jesus and his companions encounter yet another crowd, he is immediately approached by a frustrated man. The man has seen the disciples healing people, and so he brings his epileptic son to them to be healed, but nothing happens. The disciples lay hands on the boy and pray with him, but nothing happens. They pray with energy and conviction, but nothing happens. Now the man presents his boy to Jesus with a plea for mercy.

Jesus cannot contain his reaction, and he turns to his disciples and confronts them. After all he has taught them, after all they have seen, even after going out and successfully healing people, when confronted

with a difficult situation, their faith has failed them. Somehow their knowledge and experience of the power of God have succumbed to some unnamed fear or faith-killing doubt.

Jesus expects them to do as he does, but he is frustrated by their frequent inability to hold on to their faith and trust in him. He desperately wants them to be a part of what he is doing. He knows he will have to entrust his mission to them quite soon, and here they are, stumbling over their own lack of faith rather than acting in the power he has given to them.

Without missing a beat, Jesus asks to have the boy brought to him. He responds at once to the desperation of the father and the horrible situation of the son. A simple command is given, and the boy is free and well. The father's raw faith wins the moment.

Embarrassment abounds among the disciples, accompanied by looks of confusion. When the first opportunity presents itself to take Jesus aside and speak to him privately, they ask, "Why could we not heal the boy?" (cf. Matthew 17:19).

Jesus explains the problem, this time without the edge of anger and frustration he had first voiced. This time there is more a tone of regret and sadness: "Your faith is too small. If it were only the size of a mustard seed, nothing would be impossible for you" (cf. Matthew 17:20).

Across the distance of a couple of thousand years, it may seem reasonable to think, "Come on, Jesus, they were just disciples. You are the Son of God." But clearly, Jesus expected them to be acting at a level comparable to his own. Closer to home, he invites us to act at a comparable level. His declaration in the Gospel of John that those who believe in him would do the things that he does and "will do greater works than these" is a challenge for us (14:12).

In his final commission to his disciples, Jesus declares, among other things, that those who believe in him "will lay their hands on the sick, and they will recover" (Mark 16:18). How frustrated the Lord must be with a people that often fails even to attempt to act in faith and bring healing to the world!

The fact is, however, that many of us have attempted to pray with others for healing, either directly or in our own private prayer, and more often than not, we have not seen anything happen. It only takes a few such experiences to convince a person that praying for healing is simply "not my gift."

Even when we do see improvement in the health of the person we pray for or an actual healing, we tend to be more likely to remember the times when nothing at all seems to have happened.

Of course, there is a problem with the notion that "nothing seems to have happened." Very often, things do happen when we pray, but they happen slowly or in ways we did not anticipate. A whole world of transformation may be happening in the person that we have prayed for.

But what we usually mean when we say "nothing seems to have happened" is that we were asking for a direct physical result, and it did not occur.

Realistically, there will be many times when we pray with people and do not see anything happen, either in the short or long run. The great healer St. Vincent Ferrer (1350–1490) would at times pray over huge audiences with thousands of sick people. Hundreds of them would be healed, sometimes even thousands, but many more would not.

There are so many variables in any given situation that a universal cause for "failed" healing cannot be spelled out. Faith is one

component, but as we have seen, the faith may be strong in the person asking to be healed, or it may be strong in their friends, or it may be strong in the person praying for the healing.

Side by side with faith, we may find two insidious competitors: fear and doubt. We may fear that "nothing will happen," or sometimes we can be afraid that something *will* happen. We may fear that we are asking for the wrong thing. We may fear that we are being presumptuous. We may even fear praying out loud or praying for something very specific. Fear comes to us in a multitude of ways.

Of course, doubt also easily undermines faith. "Should I even be doing this?" "Who do I think I am that I could pray with this person for healing?" "Why would God work through me? I'm too great a sinner." We doubt the promises Jesus has made to be with us and to answer us. We doubt the power of the Holy Spirit. We doubt the Father's love for us and for the person we are praying for.

There are other factors that we are not able to see. God may be at work in a person in a very unique and specific way and at a particular moment in time, and healing may not be what is needed. There may be some larger purpose for what is going on that is beyond our range of understanding or vision.

So in a given instance, when we have the opportunity to pray with someone for healing, should we go ahead with it or not? The evidence and direction in Scripture seems to be that we should always pray for healing.

I've prayed with literally thousands of people. Have they all been healed when I prayed with them? No! Have many of them been healed? Yes! Many have experienced doctor-verified, knock-your-socks-off, astonishing moments of healing. Sometimes there have

been others involved in the prayer; sometimes I have been the only one praying with the person needing healing.

What has happened to those who were not healed? Some were healed later on at other people's hands. Some were healed through their medical treatment. Some simply went through the normal course of the disease or the injury and eventually became well. Some died.

Isn't it dangerous to pray with people and raise their expectations that God is going to heal them?

It certainly can be. It is possible to pressure people into thinking that if they are not healed, it will be a sign of some kind of moral failure on their part. This is clearly wrong. Jesus dealt harshly with those who tried to judge anyone who was sick.

Praying with people for healing involves walking a fine line. We don't want to undermine faith that God can heal, and we also don't want to make promises for God that he may not want to keep in the way you have chosen.

It is good to repent of fear or doubt when praying with people and to encourage them to do the same. It is good to fan into a flame whatever tiny ember of faith there is in yourself and in the person with whom you pray. Look to Jesus, look to his healing stories, look to those of the apostles in Acts. If you know healing stories, historic or current, keep track of them and use them to stir your faith and the faith of the person you pray with.

If you pray and nothing seems to happen, accept it in humility. That in itself will help the person you have prayed with. Encourage the person to get prayed with again. If another opportunity presents itself to pray with that person, do it.

I prayed weekly with my friend Joe for healing of his diabetes, which was causing vision problems and neuropathy. Every time I would see him, I would ask if he wanted me to pray with him, and every time he said, "Yes, I want the usual."

After six months of this, I was out of town when I usually would have seen him. When I returned and we got together to pray, I asked him if he wanted "the usual," and he said, "No! I didn't get to tell you. After the last time we prayed, the diabetes went away completely. My doctor is stunned because I wasn't doing well at all before. Now my eyes are great, and so is everything else."

"So what do you want prayer for then?" I asked. He told me that he had become so energetic that he got carried away doing some work around the house and broke a toe!

Understand!

1. The man came to the disciples, asking them to heal his son. Why did he expect that they could cure him? What evidence might he have had?

_____

_____

_____

_____

_____

2. What authority and commission had Jesus given to the twelve apostles (see Matthew 10:1, 5-15)? Why should the disciples have been able to heal the epileptic boy?

_____

_____

_____

_____

_____

3. Why was Jesus so frustrated with the disciples? How do his words here in Matthew contrast with what he says in Luke 10:17-20, when the seventy-two disciples return from their mission?

_____

_____

_____

_____

4. Jesus explains what the disciples' problem was in Matthew 17:20. What impact might fear and doubt have had on the disciples' faith?

_____

_____

_____

_____

5. Jesus says that faith the size of a mustard seed can move mountains. What does that say about the nature and power of faith?

_____

_____

_____

_____

▶ In the Spotlight
A Mustard Seed of Faith

We need faith, not just for healing, but also to be able to forgive. In Luke, Jesus tells his disciples that if a brother "sins against you seven times a day, and turns back to you seven times and says, 'I repent,' you must forgive" (17:4). Immediately, the disciples say to the Lord, "Increase our faith!" and Jesus replies, "If you had faith the size of a mustard seed, you could say to this mulberry tree, 'Be uprooted and planted in the sea,' and it would obey you" (17:5, 6). Scripture commentator Gayle Somers makes this observation about the passage:

> When the apostles heard that they must extend forgiveness in such an expansive (and impossible) way, they assumed they had to conjure up this kind of love themselves. If they had more faith, they could do it. By telling them that even faith the size of a mustard seed would be enough to work wonders, Jesus immediately shifts the emphasis away from the wonder-worker and onto the Worker of wonders. It is not the size of our faith but its Object that makes all the difference. If we are thinking about the size of our faith, we are thinking about ourselves. If we are thinking about the impossibility of what needs to happen, such as forgiving others endlessly, we would do well to think about God and His unlimited power. To believe that God can do anything in and through us simply takes faith. Jesus uses the metaphor of a mustard seed to emphasize that impossible things are accomplished when our faith in God—our trust in Him to hear our prayers and act on our behalf—is exercised. It is not the amount of faith that matters but its quality. Faith is the human action through which the power of God is released in the world. With

God, nothing is impossible (see Genesis 18:14; Matthew 19:26; Luke 1:37).

Grow!

1. What are your most common doubts when it comes to praying for healing, either for yourself or for someone else? What are your most common fears?

_____

_____

_____

_____

_____

2. How well do you walk the fine line between expectant faith and recognizing the fact that God may not choose to heal someone in the way you ask? How do you keep your own faith intact when you don't see the results of your prayer?

_____

_____

_____

_____

_____

3. When they do their confounding work, fear and doubt can undermine faith—even if our faith seems entirely reasonable. What are some ways to deal with fear and doubt in relationship to prayer and faith?

_____

_____

_____

_____

_____

4. Jesus promised us that our faith can move mountains. When have you seen "mountains" moved by your prayers? How did this build up your faith?

_____

_____

_____

_____

_____

5. Recall a time when you persevered in prayer and yet did not see the answers you were seeking. How did you respond? Did you see your prayers answered in a different way?

_____

_____

_____

_____

Reflect!

Spend some time with Peter in the boat in Matthew 14:22-33. Sit down beside Peter (sorry, showers were not regularly available back then—this is the way all fishermen smelled!). It's a rough crossing. The wind is against the boat and the waves are tossing it around.

Then you see Jesus walking across the lake as if he were on solid land. No one is really sure it is Jesus. Walking on water? Is it a ghost? Jesus calls out, "Take heart! It's me!" (cf. Matthew 14:27). Peter jumps up and says, "If it's you, Lord, tell me to come across the water to you, and I will" (cf. 14:28). At the last second, Peter pulls you up by the arm, and suddenly you are both out of the boat, walking on the waves. They feel like water, they look like water, but they are holding up you and Peter like solid rock. It's fine as long as the

two of you look to Jesus, but a wave suddenly splashes you, and the reality of where you are standing hits you, and down you both go.

And Jesus saves you both.

There's no need to think that your faith is so much worse than any of the "greats" in the kingdom of God. It was you *and* Peter who were getting the sinking feeling here.

Sometimes the stories we tell about the apostles and the saints are so sanitized that we can forget they were each every bit as human as you or me. When it comes down to it, many of the stories the Gospels tell about Peter and the rest of the lot are downright unflattering, and it doesn't get much better in the Acts of the Apostles.

The point is, none of us redeem ourselves. None of us save ourselves. When we think we are on our own, or that we are doing it ourselves, we are bound to sink. Life works best when lived in the Lord. That is where we will find faith strong enough to overcome fear and doubt.

Now, go for a walk on the lake with Peter again, and see if you both can get it right!

Act!

Is there anyone for whom you were praying but then stopped because nothing was happening? Start praying again. Check with those people and find out what they need or if their needs have changed at all. Keep on praying for them.

▶ In the Spotlight
Facing Death

Gary was in a battle for his life. For over a year, he had been in and out of treatment for lung cancer. Chemotherapy had given him some temporary gains against his enemy. His tumors had shrunk enough to allow surgery, and for a time it appeared that the removal of the cancerous masses would give him victory.

Gary and his wife were people of profound faith, and they prayed together daily, asking for God's mercy and healing. They also sought out the prayers of others, attending healing Masses at their parish and at other parishes as well.

Each day they found themselves more and more dependent on the Lord. They knew the treatments were taking their toll on Gary's body, and the weakness and fatigue he experienced took away many of the things they had loved doing together. Travel plans were curtailed, parties scaled back, and work around the house and yard was increasingly put in the hands of generous friends and family members.

As Gary's friends heard about his struggle, many of them wanted to offer help and support but found themselves nervous and awkward when they would talk to Gary or his wife. Gary always overcame that awkwardness. He was known for his warmth and good humor, and in his crisis those qualities became even more prominent.

When people would ask how Gary was staying so positive in the middle of so much pain and sickness and an increasingly dark prognosis, he always replied, "It's the Lord. It's his love and yours!"

As the disease gradually overwhelmed all medical options, Gary remained cheerful. He regularly asked to be prayed with for healing. He asked all of his friends to pray for that. He was ready to die, but he also was ready to live. He wanted to have more time with his wife, family, and friends.

Three of his friends offered to come and pray with him on a regular basis, and he welcomed the offer. Every time they gathered at his bedside, the room was filled with laughter and real hope.

When someone commented that he should be preparing for death rather than praying for healing, Gary smiled and said, "I'm going to ask the Lord to heal me right to the moment of my death. I'm not afraid to die, but I'm not afraid to live either."

Gary finally succumbed to his cancer. Even as he died, he did not lose hope. He knew that he was in a "win-win" situation. It would be a wonderful thing if the Lord healed him, and it would be a wonderful thing to go and be with the Lord.

Standing in that faith, Gary was not trying to escape pain and suffering. He knew from his life experience that pain of all kinds can be turned to good purpose by the Lord. He knew that in his own pain he was experiencing the suffering of Jesus and growing in understanding of the depth of Jesus' love for himself and for everyone that Gary loved. At the same time, he remained confident in the power of Jesus to heal him here and now, right to the moment of his death.

Jesus the healer did not escape suffering, pain, and death. He took it on and overcame it, but he did not escape it or try to evade it. Because his faith in the Lord never wavered, Gary shared in that victory. The people who had been praying for Gary did not find their faith lessened by Gary's death. They could see God's power at work in him, and they rejoiced in his victory.

Looking Forward

John 11:17-27, 32-44

[17] When Jesus arrived, he found that Lazarus had already been in the tomb for four days. [18] Now Bethany was near Jerusalem, some two miles away, [19] and many of the Jews had come to Martha and Mary to console them about their brother. [20] When Martha heard that Jesus was coming, she went and met him, while Mary stayed at home. [21] Martha said to Jesus, "Lord, if you had been here, my brother would not have died. [22] But even now I know that God will give you whatever you ask of him." [23] Jesus said to her, "Your brother will rise again." [24] Martha said to him, "I know that he will rise again in the resurrection on the last day." [25] Jesus said to her, "I am the resurrection and the life. Those who believe in me, even though they die, will live, [26] and everyone who lives and believes in me will never die. Do you believe this?" [27] She said to him, "Yes, Lord, I believe that you are the Messiah, the Son of God, the one coming into the world." . . .

[32] When Mary came where Jesus was and saw him, she knelt at his feet and said to him, "Lord, if you had been here, my brother would not have died." [33] When Jesus saw her weeping, and the Jews who came with her also weeping, he was greatly disturbed in spirit and deeply moved. [34] He said, "Where have you laid him?" They said to him, "Lord, come and see." [35] Jesus began to weep. [36] So the Jews said, "See how he loved him!" [37] But some of them said, "Could not he who opened the eyes of the blind man have kept this man from dying?"

[38] Then Jesus, again greatly disturbed, came to the tomb. It was a cave, and a stone was lying against it. [39] Jesus said, "Take away the stone." Martha, the sister of the dead man, said to him, "Lord, already there is a stench because he has been dead for four days." [40] Jesus said to her, "Did I not tell you that if you believed, you would see the glory of God?" [41] So they took away the stone. And Jesus looked upward and said, "Father, I thank you for having heard me.

[42] I knew that you always hear me, but I have said this for the sake of the crowd standing here, so that they may believe that you sent me." [43] When he had said this, he cried with a loud voice, "Lazarus, come out!" [44] The dead man came out, his hands and feet bound with strips of cloth, and his face wrapped in a cloth. Jesus said to them, "Unbind him, and let him go."

We arrive at this scene very late in Jesus' public ministry. Jesus has left Judea because there are many who would just as soon stone him to death. Others wait to have him arrested as a blasphemer for "making himself equal to God" (John 5:18).

A message comes to Jesus from Mary and Martha. "Our brother is seriously ill. Please come to him" (cf. John 11:3). Lazarus is a dear friend of Jesus. Jesus also cares deeply about Mary and Martha. They are among his most loyal friends, but Jesus clearly sees something else in the illness of his friend. He chooses to wait for two more days.

When he finally heads for Bethany, the disciples are alarmed. Bethany is in Judea and close to Jerusalem. It is too dangerous to go there, but Jesus senses that Lazarus is "asleep" and that he needs to "awaken him" (John 11:11). The disciples don't understand what he means and so he spells it out. Lazarus is dead, and his death is going to be an occasion for God to be glorified. The situation in Judea is bad enough that Thomas, at least, is convinced that they are all going to meet their end (11:16).

When Jesus arrives, Lazarus has already been in the tomb for four days. Lazarus was well-known, and the town is crowded with mourners. Even people from Jerusalem have come to grieve with the sisters.

Martha runs to Jesus and sadly rebukes him for not being there to save Lazarus. But she has not completely given up hope. She says that

she is certain that God will give Jesus whatever he asks for, but when Jesus tells her plainly that Lazarus will rise, she does not understand and replies, "I know that he will rise again in the resurrection on the last day" (John 11:24).

"No, Martha, I'm telling you, I am the resurrection. Whoever believes in me will never die. Do you believe this?" (cf. John 11:25-26). Martha believes, but she still is struggling to take in what Jesus is telling her. She runs to get Mary and brings her to Jesus. Many of the mourners come with Mary, thinking she is going to visit the tomb yet again. Mary kneels at Jesus' feet and weeps. She lets out the same quiet rebuke that Martha had given. "If only you had been here . . . " (cf. 11:32). The grief of his friends sweeps over Jesus. He asks where the tomb is. He, too, is in tears.

They make their way to the tomb, and Jesus tells them to remove the stone blocking its entrance. "Lord, already there is a stench," Martha says (John 11:39). Lazarus has been dead for four days. In the heat of Judea, with no real embalming practice, the time during which a corpse is being reduced to dust and bones is not a time to open a tomb. But it is done as Jesus says, and he again challenges Martha to believe.

The stone is removed. The wretched odor of death is gone! Jesus prays aloud to his Father, but not because he needs to. What is done is done, but the people need to hear so that they might believe.

Jesus calls Lazarus out of the tomb. Everything is silent. People can hardly breathe, and then there is a quiet shuffling. Bound up for his burial, Lazarus works his way through the door of the tomb. No one can move. "Well, good people, don't just stand there. Unbind him and let him go!" (cf. John 11:44).

There are only a few stories in the Gospels of people being raised from the dead. The son of the widow of Nain comes back to life, but not

with a glorified body. He is the same as he was before he died. His life has been given back to him for the sake of his widowed mother (Luke 7:11-17). Jairus' daughter does not come back to life able to walk through locked doors or looking so radiant that her parents can't recognize her. She has been brought back out of mercy for her mother and father (8:40-56). Lazarus is still the same flesh and blood that he was before he died. He is now healthy; the decay is gone, but not forever.

Those whom Jesus raises from the dead will eventually die again. These resurrections are acts of love and mercy for a season and a purpose. They are not first instances of the final great resurrection of the dead that Jesus and many other Jews believed awaited them in the distant future.

It is only when Jesus is raised from the dead that we begin to get an actual glimpse of what is yet to come. When the risen Jesus comes to his disciples, he is so radiant that they do not at first recognize him (Luke 24:15-16; John 21:4-7). Yet as he speaks to them, they do know it really is Jesus. He breaks bread with them, eats with them, and is embraced by them; and they can touch him, one even putting a finger in his wounds, which are still fully visible (Luke 24:13-49; John 20:11-29; 21:1-14). He also can apparently pass through closed doors, rapidly travel great distances, and appear or disappear in a moment. Yet he is not a ghost. If we want to know what resurrected life looks like, we need to look at Jesus after the resurrection, not at Lazarus after his "temporary" rising.

So what are we to learn from the raising of Lazarus, the widow's son, and the little girl? What is Jesus showing us?

We can make two observations about the heart of each of these stories, most particularly about the story of Lazarus. First, deep love is what motivates Jesus. Mary and Martha are people that Jesus loves

dearly. The loss of Lazarus has devastated the sisters, and he experiences their pain.

Second, these acts of raising the dead are a clear demonstration of Jesus' power and authority over all things, here and now. He can make people whole, even when death has taken them over. He really is "the resurrection and the life" (John 11:25).

Of course, such love and such power also point toward the last day, when all of us will be raised up for a final reckoning and for a transformed, eternal physical life in a new heaven and new earth. The new creation will come together in the new Jerusalem, welding together all things for the glory, praise, and honor of God. That's a vision that is hard for us to grasp and even harder to hang on to.

These stories are occasions for faith in what is yet to come.

Life as we know it is not the end. In this life we often encounter struggles, sickness, injuries to body and soul, weakness, failure, division, sin, and discouragement. In Jesus the mix is transformed. In him peace and joy can be found; healing, strength, victory over our weaknesses, and unity in love are all within our reach, even now. But like the raising of Lazarus and the others, these things are all somehow incomplete. When all things are finally gathered together in Jesus, the good things of this life will be completed, made perfect and whole.

While we are living this life, God gives us signs of the new creation that awaits us. The love that Jesus brings to us from our Father in the power of the Holy Spirit is the greatest of those signs. The gifts God gives us in the Church, such as the Eucharist, are among those signs. Healing is one of those signs. The love we experience in relationships is one of those signs.

God wants to keep us moving forward toward that new heaven and new earth that are our ultimate destination. He wants us to live lives that are in themselves an invitation to others to join us on the journey. He wants us to live lives that spill over with his love for everyone that we encounter.

Healing is not an end in itself. It is a gift that God gives us to encourage us on the road that we are following. It is one among many demonstrations of his presence with us. It is a manifestation of his love, but it is not an end in itself.

There are still stories of people being raised from the dead even in our own time. Most often they come from places where the gospel is being introduced to people that have never heard of it before, or where poverty and other circumstances have people so completely beaten down that they need dramatic signs that God is still present with them. But ultimately, even those who are raised today will die.

All of creation is good. It was all created by our good and loving God. Yet all of creation is groaning as it waits for the new creation (cf. Romans 8:22). We were given stewardship over it all, and all too often we have misused it. All too often we have hurt each other and ourselves. Sickness and death are in the world because of our own sin as well as the work of the enemy.

But God has not despaired of us. He draws us forward toward our ultimate goal in him, in which all things—including ourselves—will indeed be made new. If we let ourselves be filled with expectation, we will find more ways to bring love and healing to those along the path.

If we begin to understand God's patience with us and press on patiently ourselves, we will experience the joys and victories of those who wait for the Lord. As we step out and exercise our faith, we will find ourselves able to bring more life and love to others on

the path. Jesus has made us worthy for this road and for anything that he asks us to do while we are on it.

Even when we don't see results from our efforts—be they efforts to pray with others, or to effect changes in our own lives, or to effect changes in the world around us—we need to press on in faith, beating back fear and doubt.

Look forward. Our road leads to a destination where the ultimate healing will take place, and sickness and death will be vanquished forever. We can begin to see it even now.

Understand!

1. In an earlier part of this story (John 11:1-16), Jesus makes a deliberate choice to delay his journey to Bethany. What explanation does Jesus give for the delay? Do you think the disciples understand what he means?

   _____

   _____

   _____

   _____

   _____

2. It seems that Jesus knows exactly what he is planning to do, and yet when he meets Martha, Mary, and their friends, he joins them in weeping. What is happening here? What moves him to weep?

   _____

   _____

   _____

   _____

3. While both Martha and Mary believe that Jesus could have healed Lazarus, the text seems to suggest that neither of them really expects Jesus to be able to do anything for Lazarus once he was dead. Why?

_____

_____

_____

_____

_____

4. Why do you think Jesus prays out loud to his Father? What does this indicate about his relationship with God the Father?

_____

_____

_____

_____

_____

5. The raising of Lazarus caused many to believe in Jesus, and yet it also seemed to be the impetus behind the chief priests and Pharisees' plotting of his death (John 11:45-53). How could such a sign of Jesus' authority and power cause such opposite reactions?

_____

_____

_____

_____

_____

▶ In the Spotlight
Burying the Dead

According to Dr. Byron R. McCane, professor of religion at Wofford College, "The Lazarus narrative in John 11 accurately represents typical customs of mourning, tomb construction, and grave wrappings." Jews were buried, if at all possible, on the day they died. As soon as death was certain, the deceased's eyes were closed, and the corpse was washed and then wrapped and bound with strips of cloth. The corpse would then be carried towards the place of interment, with friends, neighbors, and relatives following in a procession. Such a procession is mentioned in the story of Jesus' raising of the son of the widow of Nain (see Luke 7:12). The procession would begin at the family home and make its way to the family tomb. Members of the family would place the body in the tomb while friends and relatives waited outside. Sometimes an area near the tomb was set aside for lamenting and eulogizing the deceased. After the burial, the procession returned to the family home, where friends and relatives continued to grieve and express their condolences for several days. After seven days, ordinary life resumed.

After a full year, there was a secondary burial. In a private ceremony, family members returned to the tomb, took the bones of the deceased from their resting place on a shelf or a niche, and placed them in an ossuary.

Grow!

1. Even though Jesus knew he could take away the burden of sorrow that Mary and Martha were experiencing, he entered into their sorrow before he took away its cause. How could that approach affect the way you might pray with someone for healing?

   _____

   _____

   _____

   _____

   _____

2. What do you hope life will be like after the resurrection of the body, to which we profess belief in the Creed? What insights can you gain from meditating on stories of Jesus' resurrection?

   _____

   _____

   _____

   _____

   _____

3. What are some things that you experience now that are signs of the new creation that awaits all of us? How is the Eucharist a sign?

   _____

   _____

   _____

   _____

4. What specific practices are most helpful for you in times of doubt and discouragement? Which Scripture passages and stories have helped you to see beyond your trials to the promises of God?

_____

_____

_____

_____

_____

5. What can you do, practically as well as spiritually, to keep your ultimate destination more in focus?

_____

_____

_____

_____

_____

Reflect!

Read through the story of Lazarus and ask the Lord to open up this story for you. Choose one of the main characters and walk through the story with that person. Use your imagination to see the places in which the story is happening. Smell the smells and feel the wind or the heat or the dry, dusty air. Pay attention to people's faces. What do you see in their eyes, in their reactions? What kind of quiet gossip is going on in the background? Look at Jesus. Pay attention to the way he responds, not only to people, but to the situation he finds them in.

Let yourself react to what you are seeing. What do you feel when Lazarus shuffles out of the tomb and then when he is freed from his bindings and found to be completely healthy?

Talk to Jesus about what you see, and then have a conversation with him about what he wants you to know about himself through this story.

Act!

Think about people you know who are dealing with an ongoing illness. It could be someone you work with, someone in your neighborhood, or someone in your parish. Make a list, and then pray regularly for each person.

Then select someone from the list who seems to be having a particularly difficult time. Contact that person. Visit him or her. Ask what he needs the most on a practical level. If possible, offer to fill that need. Ask as well if you might pray with him for healing. If he agrees, do it!

▶ In the Spotlight
The Church's Healing Gifts

The Church offers us a powerhouse of healing gifts. The Sacrament of Anointing of the Sick is sometimes administered in the context of Mass but can be given at home or in a hospital room. For most of the major surgeries I've had, I received the Anointing of the Sick beforehand, and at least one time a hospital chaplain anointed me during my recovery "to help me along."

The Sacrament of Reconciliation has been known to bring physical healing with it, as has the Anointing of the Sick. These two sacraments are called "the sacraments of healing" by the *Catechism*, which notes,

The Lord Jesus Christ, physician of our souls and bodies, who forgave the sins of the paralytic and restored him to bodily health (cf. Mark 2:1-12), has willed that his Church continue, in the power of the Holy Spirit, his work of healing and salvation, even among her own members. This is

the purpose of the two sacraments of healing: the sacrament of Penance and the sacrament of Anointing of the Sick. (1421)

Of course, the Eucharist, that incredibly intimate encounter with Jesus, has a long history of healings and miracles attached to it.

Other healing services, be they sacramental or not, are also often powerful moments of God's action. "Where two or three are gathered" in his name (Matthew 18:20), the Lord is present and wanting to act.

Practical Pointers for Bible Discussion Groups

A Bible discussion group is another key that can help us unlock God's word. Participating in a discussion or study group—whether through a parish, a prayer group, or a neighborhood—offers us the opportunity to grow not only in our love for God's word but also in our love for one another. We don't have to be trained Scripture scholars to benefit from discussing and studying the Bible together. Bible study groups provide environments in which we can worship and pray together and strengthen our relationships with other Christians. The following guidelines can help a group get started and run smoothly.

Getting Started

- Decide on a regular time and place to meet. Meeting on a regular basis allows the group to maintain continuity without losing momentum from the previous discussion.

- Set a time limit for each session. An hour and a half is a reasonable length of time in which to have a rewarding discussion on the material contained in each of the sessions in this guide. However, the group may find that a longer time is even more advantageous. If it is necessary to limit the meeting to an hour, select sections of the material that are of greatest interest to the group.

- Designate a moderator or facilitator to lead the discussions and keep the meetings on schedule. This person's role is to help preserve good group dynamics by keeping the discussion on track. He or she should help ensure that no one monopolizes the session and that each person—including the shyest or quietest

individual—is offered an opportunity to speak. The group may want to ask members to take turns moderating the sessions.

- Provide a copy of the study for each member of the group, and ask everyone to bring a Bible to the meetings. Each session's Scripture text and related passages for reflection are printed in full in the guides, but you will find that a Bible is helpful for looking up other passages and cross-references. The translation provided in this guide is the New Revised Standard Version (Catholic Edition). You may also want to refer to other translations—for example, the New American Bible or the New Jerusalem Bible—to gain additional insights into the text.

- Try to stay faithful to your commitment and attend as many sessions as possible. Not only does regular participation provide coherence and consistency to the group discussions, but it also demonstrates that members value one another and are committed to sharing their lives with one another.

Session Dynamics

- Read the material for each session in advance and take time to consider the questions and your answers to them. The single most important key to any successful Bible study is having everyone prepared to participate.

- As a courtesy to all members of your group, try to begin and end each session on schedule. Being prompt respects the other commitments of the members and allows enough time for discussion. If the group still has more to discuss at the end of the allotted time, consider continuing the discussion at the next meeting.

- Open the sessions with prayer. A different person could have the responsibility of leading the opening prayer at each session.

The prayer could be a spontaneous one, a traditional prayer such as the Our Father, or one that relates to the topic of that particular meeting. The members of the group might also want to begin some of the meetings with a song or hymn. Whatever you choose, ask the Holy Spirit to guide your discussion and study of the Scripture text presented in that session.

- Contribute actively to the discussion. Let the members of the group get to know you, but try to stick to the topic so that you won't divert the discussion from its purpose. And resist the temptation to monopolize the conversation so that everyone will have an opportunity to learn from one another.

- Listen attentively to everyone in the group. Show respect for the other members and their contributions. Encourage, support, and affirm them as they share. Remember that many questions have more than one answer and that the experience of everyone in the group can be enriched by considering a variety of viewpoints.

- If you disagree with someone's observation or answer to a question, do so gently and respectfully, in a way that shows that you value the person who made the comment, and then explain your own point of view. For example, rather than saying, "You're wrong!" or "That's ridiculous!" try something like "I think I see what you're getting at, but I think that Jesus was saying something different in this passage." Be careful to avoid sounding aggressive or argumentative. Then watch to see how the subsequent discussion unfolds. Who knows? You may come away with a new and deeper perspective.

- Don't be afraid of pauses and reflective moments of silence during the session. People may need some time to think about a question before putting their thoughts into words.

- Maintain and respect confidentiality within the group. Safeguard the privacy and dignity of each member by not repeating what has been shared during the discussion session unless you have been given permission to do so. That way everyone will get the greatest benefit out of the group by feeling comfortable enough to share on a deep, personal level.

- End the session with prayer. Thank God for what you have learned through the discussion, and ask him to help you integrate it into your life.

The Lord blesses all our efforts to come closer to him. As you spend time preparing for and meeting with your small group, be confident in the knowledge that Christ will fill you with wisdom, insight, grace, and the ability to see him at work in your daily life.

Sources and Acknowledgments

Session 3: Faith, Wherever It Can Be Found

Xavier Léon-Dufour, *Dictionary of Biblical Theology* (Frederick, MD: The Word Among Us Press, Inc., 1995), 37.

Session 4: Who Is Worthy?

Flavius Vegetius Renatus, *De Re Militari*, trans. John Clarke, II.14, accessed at http://www.digitalattic.org/home/war/vegetius/index.php#b203.

Session 5: When There Is No Healing

Gayle Somers, "Scripture Speaks: Faith of Mustard Seed," *Catholic Exchange*, October 7, 2013, accessed at http://catholicexchange.com/ scripture-speaks-faith-of-a-mustard-seed.

Session 6: Looking Forward

Byron R. McCane, "Burial Practices in First Century Palestine," Bible Odyssey, accessed at http://www.bibleodyssey.org/en/people/related-articles/burial-practices-in-first-century-palestine.

The Word Among Us
Keys to the Bible Series
For Individuals or Groups

These studies open up the meaning of the Scriptures while placing each passage within the context of the Bible and Church tradition.

Each of the six sessions feature

- The Scripture text to be studied and insightful commentary
- Questions for reflection, discussion, and personal application
- "In the Spotlight" sections that offer wisdom from the saints, personal testimony, and fascinating historical background

Here are just a few of our popular titles:

 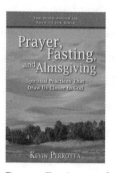 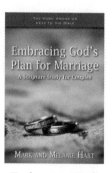 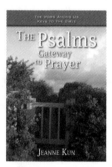

| Treasures Uncovered: The Parables of Jesus | Prayer, Fasting, and Almsgiving | Embracing God's Plan for Marriage | The Psalms: Gateway to Prayer |

Check out all the studies available in this series
by going online at **bookstore.wau.org**
or
call Customer Service at **1-800-775-9673**

the WORD
among us®
The *Spirit* of Catholic Living

This book was published by The Word Among Us. Since 1981, The Word Among Us has been answering the call of the Second Vatican Council to help Catholic laypeople encounter Christ in the Scriptures.

The name of our company comes from the prologue to the Gospel of John and reflects the vision and purpose of all of our publications: to be an instrument of the Spirit, whose desire is to manifest Jesus' presence in and to the children of God. In this way, we hope to contribute to the Church's ongoing mission of proclaiming the gospel to the world so that all people would know the love and mercy of our Lord and grow more deeply in their faith as missionary disciples.

Our monthly devotional magazine, *The Word Among Us*, features meditations on the daily and Sunday Mass readings, and currently reaches more than one million Catholics in North America and another half million Catholics in one hundred countries around the world. Our book division, The Word Among Us Press, publishes numerous books, Bible studies, and pamphlets that help Catholics grow in their faith.

To learn more about who we are and what we publish, log on to our website at www.wau.org. There you will find a variety of Catholic resources that will help you grow in your faith.

Embrace His Word, Listen to God . . .

www.wau.org